The Computers
of *Star Trek*

The **Computers** of *Star Trek*

Lois H. Gresh
Robert Weinberg

BASIC
BOOKS

A Member of the Perseus Books Group

Published by Basic Books,
A Member of the Perseus Books Group

Designed by Rachel Hegarty

Library of Congress Cataloguing-in-Publication Data
Gresh, Lois H.
The computers of Star Trek / Lois H. Gresh, Robert Weinberg.
    p.   cm.
    ISBN 0-465-01299-X
  1. Star Trek television programs—Miscellanea. 2. Star Trek films—
Miscellanea. 3. Computers. I. Weinberg, Robert E. II Title.

PNI992.8.S74 G74   1999
791.45'75—dc21   99-042226

   01 02 03 /RRD 10 9 8 7 6 5 4 3 2 1

Dedicated with love to my parents, Sam and Freda Goldberg.

Lois H. Gresh

To Dr. Marshall Sparberg and
Dr. Karen Spurgash—the best doctors
I've ever met.

Robert Weinberg

Contents

The authors thank Larry Charet of Chicago, who made available to us his video library of every episode of all the *Star Trek* television shows as well as the *Star Trek* movies. Without his help, this book would not have been possible. Thanks also to our agent, Lori Perkins, her associate, Susan Rabiner, and our editor, Bill Frucht, for reasons too many to mention.

Acknowledgments

Since its beginnings in the nineteenth century with the writings of Shelly, Verne and Wells, science fiction has always tried to describe what might be, what could happen, what life will be like in times to come. Unlike all other fiction, it's not concerned (at least overtly) with what exists now but what will happen later.

In 1966, the most popular science-fiction television show ever, *Star Trek*, sent its crew on an ongoing mission to explore new worlds and seek out new civilizations. A third of a century later that mission continues with new starships and new crewmembers but the same dream. Our fascination with the future remains unquenched and it seems quite possible that viewers will still be watching *Star Trek* when voyages into outer space are daily occurrences.

Intelligent plotting, combined with vivid attention to detail, makes the *Star Trek* universe the most complex future world ever created. It's a setting that's been described in more than five hundred hours of television and movies, a half-dozen computer games, a detailed chronology, and an encyclopedia. It has its own

Preface

language, Klingon, and dozens of international fan conventions. A vast number of novels have been published featuring characters from the various shows. There are *Star Trek* trivia books, photo books, postcard albums, and several technical manuals. Books have been written about the physics, the biology, and even the philosophy of *Star Trek*.

Not surprisingly, events taking place in the universe of *Star Trek*, three hundred and fifty years from now, are strikingly similar to incidents in our everyday world. This is not only because good storytelling reflects universal human concerns that do not go away with changes in technology (although, as science fiction keeps reminding us, they constantly re-emerge in new guises). The real reason for the similarity is that, after all, no science fiction can do more than project into the future the concerns of the time in which it was written. Every word, every image, every moment of every episode of *Star Trek* depicts ideas that, by definition, already exist.

It's especially important to remember this when examining, as we do in this book, the way *Star Trek* deals with computer technology. The world of the twenty-third century as envisioned by the original series is based on the technology and culture of the 1960s. The universe of *The Next Generation* is vastly different, considering the scientific and social changes that took place in the two decades following the first adventures. Today's adventures, *Deep Space Nine* and *Voyager*, reflect even greater changes that have occurred in the past decade.

These incredible advances are no better demonstrated than in the evolution of computers in the various shows. The giant thinking machines of the original series seem laughably primitive compared to the smaller and much more versatile hand-held units of the 1980s' *Next Generation*. Just as the computers of *The Next Generation* seem archaic when compared to those on *Voy-*

ager. As our world changes, so does our view of the future world of *Star Trek.* In a sense, each series is a photograph of tomorrow taken with a camera firmly rooted in today.

Will the universe of *Star Trek* ever come to pass? The answer is clear: it won't. To understand why, you need only look at the shows of the original series and think about how much we'd need to forget in order to build a world like that. But by showing you how each series reflects the ideas and technologies of its time—and even the current shows are years behind what's happening in the research labs—we hope to get you thinking about how unimaginably different the real future is going to be.

For brevity, we have used the following abbreviations to refer to episodes of the various *Star Trek* television series:

The Original Series	TOS
The Next Generation	TNG
Deep Space Nine	DS9
Voyager	VGR

Although the words *Star Trek* are formally part of all the movie titles (e.g., *Star Trek—Insurrection*), we use only the latter part of the title (*Insurrection*) except where necessary to avoid confusion.

Since this book is the collaboration of two authors, the plural *we* represents the authors' joint viewpoint. (We definitely don't have delusions of royalty.)

A Note on the Abbreviations

The Computers
of *Star Trek*

Footsteps into the Future

In the *Deep Space Nine* episode "One Little Ship," Chief O'Brien and Dr. Julian Bashir shrink to perhaps finger size and enter the computer consoles of the starship *Defiant*, trying to find a security protocol interlink. Once inside the computer, they sit on "benches" (which could well be live circuits!), wander among flashing lights reminiscent of LEDs (light-emitting diodes), and then become lost. They manage to find their goal only by using a large isolinear chip as a landmark. Moving huge pieces of hardware around like packing crates, they fix the security interlink. Then they get back into a shuttlecraft, also proportionately shrunk, and fire on some big lizardlike aliens, killing them. The *Defiant* is saved.

Of course all this is absurd. The *Star Trek* computers will have components the size of large molecules (many of their components undoubtedly *are* large molecules). If O'Brien and Bashir are as big as cockroaches, what exactly are they shoving around? What are those flashing lights for? For that matter, why does the bridge have physical consoles at all instead of virtual-reality projections?

The universe of *Star Trek* is a paradise of computers. They're everywhere and do just about everything. They're the glue that binds the entire *Star Trek* phenomenon together. Without them, everything else collapses into sheer fantasy. Without computers, this future civilization would vanish.

It's the computers—and everything they make possible—that make *Star Trek* seem like a show about the future, our future. But how believable is it really? Are these machines actually attainable, and are the tasks they perform possible? Or is much of what we see a sham, a future built on magic and sleight-of-hand, a universe that could only exist on the screen and never in real life? Most intriguing of all, will the *Star Trek* future fail to happen not because the technology is too outlandish, but because it's not outlandish enough?

As we watch *Star Trek*, we often feel like O'Brien and Bashir. We stumble around, trying to feel as if we're in the twenty-fourth century, but we keep tripping over components that look like leftovers from an old Heathkit catalogue. In part this is testament to *Star Trek*'s success. It's only because the show is so interesting and fun to watch that it's jarring to be reminded we're not looking at the real twenty-fourth century, only at a twentieth-century drama that, like all science fiction, is more about the present than the future.

Each *Star Trek* series reflects a distinct mindset, a projection into the future of the beliefs and concerns of the era in which it was produced. Thus the original series universe of the twenty-third century, as imagined in the late 1960s, is a much different place from the twenty-fourth-century cosmos visualized in the late 1980s and 1990s. *The Next Generation* was literally the next generation of TV science fiction, and nowhere is this generational difference more apparent than in the characters' attitudes about computers.

Computers are everywhere in the later programs. The *Enterprise* computer is without question the most important system on the ship—as it is on *Voyager* and every other starship in the *Star Trek* universe. Computers are at the heart of *Deep Space Nine* and every other artificial environment. From what little has been shown of life on various Federation planets, as well as the lives of Federation allies and enemies, computers are apparently critical everywhere. The population of an entire world, Bynaus, is so closely tied to the planetary computer that its failure signals the end of all life. ("11001001," *TNG*)

The *Enterprise* crew in *The Next Generation* is surrounded by computers and relies on them for everything from food to information to communication to entertainment. The crew even lives with a sentient computer—Data—in its midst.

Every sentient being in the universe of the twenty-fourth century is computer literate. Episodes of *Deep Space Nine* that show Keiko O'Brien's school, as well as *Next Generation* stories featuring Worf's son, Alexander, show young children using computers as part of their earliest education. Crewmembers on all of the starships carry PADDs (personal access display devices), handheld computers that provide instant networking to the ship's main computer core. In the current shows, being comfortable with computers isn't merely important or even necessary: It's inseparable from being a functioning member of society.

That's not nearly as true in the original series. In those adventures, the original *Enterprise*'s life-support, weapons, and navigation systems are obviously run by a central computer. This mainframe processes data gathered from the sensors and tricorders, serves as a huge storehouse of information, and even analyzes difficult social problems ("A Piece of the Action," *TOS*). Yet despite the machine's importance to the ship, a strong distrust of computers is woven into many of the original series' episodes.

The late 1960s were a period of great economic and social change in the United States. It was a time when America's most powerful enemy was a nation in which the ideals of rational order and control had produced a nightmarish, dehumanizing society. The ease with which utopia could shade into dystopia was a major concern for science-fiction writers. Computers were like fire: powerful tools if kept firmly under control. Several episodes reflect the concern that the absolutely rational, collectivist values of the computer would take over and subjugate human freedom.

The Vulcan science officer, Mr. Spock, with his totally logical approach to life, and Dr. McCoy, the emotional humanist, represented the extreme cases for and against computer technology. Captain Kirk occupied the middle ground, relying on both Spock and McCoy for guidance. Clearly, a balanced path between the ideologies was the right choice.

For example, in "The Conscience of the King," Kirk suspects that an actor, Anton Karidian, is in reality the notorious Kodos the Executioner, a mass murderer presumed dead for the past twenty years. Spock and Kirk use the ship's computer to conduct a thorough investigation of the massacre for which Kodos was responsible. They soon discover that most of the witnesses to the disaster have died under mysterious circumstances over the years. Each death took place when Karidian's theater company was nearby.

Kirk refuses to be swayed by circumstantial evidence. Instead, he orders a sound scan made of the actor's voice and instructs the computer to compare the recording with one of Kodos' speeches. The computer states that the two voices are identical.

Despite this evidence, the captain still refuses to act. He's unwilling to trust a machine's judgment when a man's life is at stake. So much for twenty-third-century technology.

When Captain Kirk is brought to trial for killing one of his crew in "Court Martial," the Board of Review studying the computer transcripts has no such qualms. They know beyond doubt that computers don't lie. However, Kirk's lawyer, Samuel T. Cogley, puts his trust in law books instead of computer records because, he tells Kirk, the books contain much more detailed information. Cogley's defense of Kirk consists of angrily declaring that computer evidence isn't enough to prove a man guilty. He argues his point "in the name of humanity fading before the machine."

This mistrust of computer technology is a recurring theme of the original series. In "The Return of the Archons," Kirk and his crew battle Landru, a giant thinking machine that's frozen a planet's society without change for thousands of years to protect the inhabitants from any possible danger. The theme is similar in "The Apple," in which the immense computer, Vaal, maintains an Eden-like environment for a handful of servants who in return keep it supplied with raw materials. In "The Ultimate Computer," a near-omniscient computer is given control of the *Enterprise* during space-war games to prove it can outperform the ship's human crew. Resulting, of course, in disaster.

When *Star Trek* first appeared, in 1966, computers were less than a quarter-century old. Even in the mid-1970s, those of us who were teenage programmers weren't allowed in the "computer room." We gave our coding sheets to an engineer who sat behind a bullet-proof glass window. Behind him, huge machines hummed and roared, churned giant magnetic tapes, and spat hardcopies from clanking printers onto the floor. More than anything, we wanted to get behind the glass window, touch the computers, and see how they really worked. But only the elite, the engineers of the computer room, were allowed to serve the godlike machines. The original series computers shared this mystical quality. Massive and unpredictable, they exerted their powers in accordance with inhuman, universal laws.

The first generation of computers (1945–1956), developed during World War II, were basically huge collections of on/off switches. When grouped together, these switches represented numbers that were then manipulated to solve mathematical problems. Computers were used by the United States Navy, for instance, to create ballistic charts for aiming artillery. The actual switches for these computers were vacuum tubes—large glass tubes in which electric current passed freely between metal wires. *On* was when electrons were flowing in the tube. *Off* was when they were not. On paper these two positions were represented by the numbers 1 and 0. Each switch was called a bit.

Eight bits grouped together—forming a sequence of zeros and ones—were called a byte. A row of eight bits could form 2^8 or 256 unique strings of ones and zeros. There were enough bytes to represent an entire alphabet, as well as numeric digits and punctuation marks. Bytes soon became the standard unit of measurement of computer storage.

Because bytes represent such a small amount of information, computer storage is usually described in kilobytes (2^{10} or 1024 bytes), megabytes (1024 kilobytes = 2^{20} = 1,048,576 bytes), or gigabytes (1024 megabytes). A gigabyte contains approximately ten billion bits, or individual switches. The world of computers involves very large numbers. Today, computer storage is escalating into the terabytes—trillions of bytes.

Working with first-generation computers, engineers were able to perform detailed mathematical calculations by using hundreds or sometimes thousands of vacuum tubes. ENIAC, completed in 1946 by scientists at the University of Pennsylvania, contained over 18,000 vacuum tubes and 70,000 resistors, and used over 160 kilowatts of electricity each time it was turned on. With each tube representing one bit, ENIAC thus had a capacity of 18,000 bits.

These primitive vacuum-tube computers were huge. They filled large buildings, generated intense heat, and consumed vast amounts of energy. Running ENIAC dimmed the lights in a large section of Philadelphia. Immense computers were a staple of science fiction of this period. The Krell computer in the movie *Forbidden Planet* was a first-generation computer, as was the computer in *Colossus: The Forbin Project*. The bigger the machine, the more powerful the electronic brain. Or so it seemed.

The year 1948 marked the invention of the transistor by three scientists at Bell Labs. Transistors were solid-state semiconductors that could do the work of a vacuum tube. Basically, transistors are tiny electrical components with a base, collector, and emitter connection. The voltage between the base and emitter determines whether electricity flows or is blocked between the emitter and the collector. In essence, a transistor is no more than a miniature on/off switch, dependent on electrical current. Transistors are just thousandths of an inch wide, and they completely revolutionized electronics.

The switch from vacuum tubes to transistors led to what was called the second generation of computers (1956–1963). These machines were much smaller, faster, and more energy efficient.

Equally important, second-generation computers used stored programs, in which the instructions to run the machine for a certain function were inside the computer's memory and could quickly be replaced by another set of instructions for a different function. First-generation computers could not solve more than one type of problem without placing instruction sequences into the computer along with the numeric data. Stored programs made computers versatile.

Another advance in second-generation computers was the development of programming languages. These languages, including COBOL and FORTRAN, replaced the zeros and ones (the binary code) of first-generation machines with words, numbers, and instructions. Developing specific programs for these machines led to the development of the software industry.

The computers featured on the original series are first- and second-generation machines—projected three hundred years into the future. Thus on the original *Enterprise*, specific computers handle specific problems—the ship has a library computer, a science computer, a translator computer, and a computer used for navigation. "Futuristic" means they work at incredible speeds and contain vast amounts of information. Many of them are extremely large. Like their primitive ancestors, when pressed to their limits, the machines tend to overheat. Landru, for example, self-destructs in a thick cloud of smoke.

Though larger and faster than the computers of the 1960s, the original series computers display little imagination or innovation in their basic design. Many of them print answers in machine language that have to be translated. Although most original series computers understand English (and even translate languages from alien cultures into English), most can't handle simple graphic displays. They are artificially intelligent in that they understand questions, but they are extremely limited in extrapolating data and reaching conclusions. These computers represent the future as envisioned through a narrow tunnel from the past.

The problem of computer overheating was solved in the real world by the development of a third generation of computers (1964–1971), which used silicon chips for transistors. The first integrated circuits, invented in 1958, combined three transistors on a single chip. This was quickly followed by the packing of tens, hundreds, and later thousands of transistors onto one chip. The smaller the transistor, the less distance electricity had to travel and the faster it worked. As component size shrank and more and more transistors were squeezed onto a single chip, computers became faster and smaller.

Third-generation computers also featured operating systems, which allowed a machine to run a number of different programs at the same time. Second-generation machines had only been able to work on one problem after another. In third-generation machines, the operating system acted as a central program that monitored and managed all operations of the computer. For the first time, computers were able to do multiple tasks simultaneously, which greatly increased their problem-solving speed.

As integrated circuits spread, the main direction in computer technology was smaller, faster, cheaper. The fourth generation of computers (1971–now) began with one of the breakthrough inventions of the twentieth century, the microprocessor. In 1971, the Intel 4004 chip contained all the computer's components (CPU, memory, and input/output controls). This first microprocessor contained 2,300 transistors and performed about 60,000 calculations in a second. It was manufactured in quantity and then separately programmed for all types of functions.

Soon, computers were everywhere—in televisions, automobiles, watches, microwave ovens, coffeemakers, toys, cash registers, airplanes, telephone systems, electric power grids, and stock market tickers.

Steady improvements in photolithography—the method used to etch circuits onto chips—pushed component sizes even smaller, resulting in faster computer speeds. The smaller the component, the faster a signal traveled between transistors. Large-scale integration (LSI) fit hundreds of transistors onto a chip about half the size of a dime. In the 1980s, VLSI (very large-scale integration) fit hundreds of thousands of components onto a chip. ULSI (ultra-large-scale integration) increased that number into the millions. In 1995, approximately 3.1 million transistors could be fit onto a single square-inch chip (Intel's Pentium chip). Modern microprocessors contain as many as twenty million transistors and perform hundreds of millions of calculations per second. A computer with the power of ENIAC, with its 18,000 vacuum tubes, could today fit onto a chip smaller than the period that finishes this sentence.

Industry experts estimate that there are more than 15 billion microprocessors in use today. Without them, telephones would still have rotary dials, TVs would have knobs instead of remotes, ATMs wouldn't exist, and thousands of other facets of modern life wouldn't work. Nor would an unmanned probe have walked on Mars, sending us pictures of another planet's landscape.

Equally important, microprocessors enabled computer companies to manufacture computers for home use. In 1981, IBM introduced its Personal Computer (PC) for the home, office, and schools. Today, along with at least half a billion PCs, we have laptops and handheld computers: Palm Pilots, Newtons, a multitude of tiny computers that netsurf for us.

On the original *Star Trek*, the communicators looked like today's handheld computers. The etch-a-sketch-sized pads used by Captain Kirk to sign instructions, letters, and invoices (while he ogled Yeoman Rand in her miniskirt and cracked jokes about "the pleasures of shore leave") were larger and clunkier than today's powerful handheld computers. But the use of those pads by Kirk and crew exhibited an astonishing foresight.

Kirk and his crew also used what look like today's desktop PCs to access databases, communicate with each other, and analyze sensor information. But the most amazing example of the original series' foresight is that crewmembers routinely gave each other data on disks that look exactly like today's floppy disks.

While much of the original series reflected the machines and cultural paranoia of the 1960s, the show also provided a remarkable glimpse of technology in the 1980s. Looking twenty-years ahead is a far cry from looking 300 years into the future, of course, but it's probably the best that can be expected.

Just as Kirk's computers reflected the thinking of the 1960s, the *TNG, VGR,* and *DS9* computers reflect today's thinking. They incorporate much of today's best computer science research: redundant architectures, neural nets, top-down as well as bottom-up artificial intelligence, nanotechnology, and virtual reality.

This creates some problems. For example, the *Trek* computers are outlandish in design and concept. They supposedly run faster than the speed of light, which defies the laws of physics. Though starships travel at warp speed, they actually are warping space, using the fourth-dimensional curvature of space time to achieve faster-than-light (FTL) speeds. Nothing in this theory (which is discussed at great length in *The Physics of Star Trek* by Lawrence M. Krauss [Basic Books, 1995] and is speculative at best) justifies the concept of electrons in circuits moving at FTL speeds.

The computers have a redundant architecture to handle system failures, yet constantly fail. They enable holographic doctors to hit humans and to fall in love. The *Deep Space Nine* computer is so argumentative and obstinate that Chief O'Brien must put it into manual override to save the space station from blowing up. Yet the same computer requires constant supervision, repair, and instructions from human engineers; in other words, it's not particularly intelligent by today's standards.

Then there's Data. He runs on some sort of advanced neural network (his positronic brain), but he also shows distinct signs of traditional *if-then* artificial intelligence—witness his love of Sherlock Holmes and his Spocklike deductive powers. And while he's so advanced that no human seems capable of creating another Datalike creature, Data can't interface with the ship's main computer unless somebody takes off his "skins" (the word for the cases that house today's computers, but in Data's case the hair-and-skin flap on the back of his head), does some tweaking with a screwdriver or wrench, inserts what appears to be a serial cable, and watches dozens of flashing lights in Data's skull. (See, for example, "Cause and Effect," *TNG*.) Sometimes a crewmember even has to remove Data's entire head to create the interface. ("Disaster," *TNG*)

The flashing lights harken back to the days when we gazed at blinking LEDs, jotted down which ones were off and on, and then calculated the corresponding hexadecimal values; these values meant something to us, such as ERROR 1320: MEMORY CORRUPTION. It's silly to think that Data's head hundreds of years from now will have hexadecimal LEDs to indicate SUCCESS and ERROR. The method is outdated today.

The *Star Trek* future comes to us courtesy of computer technology. However, we believe that computers will go far beyond the stuff of *Star Trek*. Tomorrow's computers will be invisible, highly intelligent, and almost lifelike. Nanotechnology and cybernetic implants will be commonplace. We'll talk to computers that are in our winter coats and in our summer sandals. Our computers will anticipate what we want before we even ask them. We'll get ticked off when our computers forget to download our digital newspaper subscriptions, make our morning toast, or automatically design clothes to fit our exact body dimensions and fashion tastes. We'll forget that computers are computers.

Getting to this point will require breakthroughs as amazing as the microprocessor. Fortunately, computer scientists are already on the job.

Since the 1950s, something called Moore's Law has loosely defined the growth in our computing power. Originally stated in 1965 by Gordon Moore, a co-founder of Intel, it maintains that the number of components that can be put on a computer chip doubles every eighteen months while the price remains the same. Essentially, this means that computer power doubles every eighteen months. (Interestingly, in a 1997 interview with *USA Today*,

Moore says that he originally stated the number of components would double every year. And that in 1971, he revised that to every two years. Eighteen months was never mentioned.)

As transistors have become smaller, Moore's Law has held with remarkable consistency. But there's a limit to how small we can make tomorrow's transistors. The limitation has to do with the wavelength of light that's used to etch circuits on silicon chips. Light beams imprint etching patterns into the silicon, and then gases carve the circuitry according to the patterns. So the circuit can't be narrower than the wavelength of light.

Mercury light beams, for example, are as tiny as one-half or one-third of a micron (one millionth of a meter). Light beams from a pulsed excimer laser may someday etch circuits with wavelengths of one-fifth of a micron.

But, and it's a big but, we can't reduce silicon circuits below one-tenth of a micron. At that size, quantum mechanics kick in and make the circuitry undependable. New techniques are essential.

It's long been postulated that gallium arsenide will replace silicon as the substrate for chips. (A substrate is a "backbone" supporting the circuits.) This new technology will help a little, but it won't get us to the world of *Star Trek*: optical isolinear circuitry that breaks the laws of the universe! How far-fetched then is a computer that operates on nothing more than beams of light?

Eight years ago, Bell Labs created an optical transistor, called the Symmetric Self-Electro-Optic Effect, a name that could be straight out of *Star Trek*. Optics are becoming fundamental to computers today. Hence the notions of *Star Trek*'s optical data network and optical isolinear chips—central pieces of the architecture of the *Enterprise* computer that we'll describe in the next chapter—are extensions of what exists in our own world.

Basically, an optical computer has a filter that either blocks light or lets it through. When the filter lets light through, we have a binary one. Otherwise we have a binary zero. We split a laser beam, putting information on one of the two "strands." Then we cross the strands, forming light patterns at the juncture. If we cross the strands at various angles and in different sections of the holographic crystal structure, we can store tons of information: literally thousands of pages of data. To read the data, we shine a laser through the holographic structure. This "reading" laser produces another light beam that displays a holographic image of the stored information.

It's thought that holographic structures will someday store hundreds of billions of bytes. This method alone makes the vast storage capacity of the *Enterprise* seem possible. But with holographic storage, we won't need the hard drives of mega-monster computers. We'll need only a tiny holographic crystal structure. Lambertus Hesselink, a computer scientist at Stanford University and chairman of the holographic research firm Optitek, believes that one holographic structure the size of a sugar cube may be able to hold a terabyte of data. With continued refinement of the holographic process, in several decades that same sugar cube will someday hold as much information as every computer in the entire world does today.[1]

Current thinking is that the merging of optical computers with holographic methods will yield the next major computer revolution.

Amazing! And straight out of *Star Trek*.

A Twenty-Fourth-Century Mainframe

The computer revolution today is a little more than a half-century old. The microprocessor has been in use for only a few decades. Yet in these few decades the computer has changed radically, from a fragile, room-sized agglomeration of vacuum tubes to a tiny chip embedded in automobile dashboards, wristwatches, and even greeting cards. It's also become embedded in our lives. What computers are and how we relate to them has changed just as radically as their physical form.

This has happened in just a generation; what will computers be like in 300 years?

Three hundred years is a *long* time from now. If we really want to visualize the future, we need to shake ourselves loose of the assumptions of today.

With that thought in mind, let's examine the most important component of any *Star Trek* spaceship—and therefore the most important piece of technology in the entire *Star Trek* universe: the ship's main computer system. The computer is responsible for the operation of all other systems on the ship, from life support to

navigation to entertainment. We have as our guide to this extraordinary machine the *Star Trek: The Next Generation—Technical Manual*,[1] whose authors compare the *Enterprise* computer to the nervous system of a human being. Let's see if it's a vision of the future.

When analyzing a computer design, a good first step is to understand its overall structure. For example, does one computer control everything, feeding tasks to workstations? Or do many computers operate in parallel? How are all the components interconnected, and what kind of networking is used? These are basic questions. Once we know the answers, the next step is to identify the underlying modules and their interconnections. In other words, we break the general design into pieces, and then we take a look at the details.*

The technical manual devotes only five pages to the *Enterprise* computer. Based on its vague and sketchy description, we've inferred the general design shown in Figure 2.1.

There are five elements here: the library computer access and retrieval software (LCARS, an acronym that you can occasionally see flash on the screen in some episodes, as if it were proprietary

---

* This is standard practice for engineers and programmers. To create hardware, we start with a general design, and draw our vision as a high-level engineering schematic. Then we break the schematic into components, and draw a more detailed blueprint for each one. We continue to subdivide the design into smaller components and to draw more detailed blueprints. Eventually, we have a roadmap to the entire system, from the outer skins and the chassis to the circuits. To create software, we do the same thing. First we write a general design that defines the main software modules (for example, one for financial accounting, another for accounts payable, and so forth). Then we break each module into components and describe such items as input, output, pointers, public or private, main tasks, required files, relationships among modules. The detailed design explicitly states how records are created, sorted, archived, deleted, and shipped over the network. It defines how each software function will be coded.

A Twenty-Fourth-Century Mainframe

FIGURE 2.1

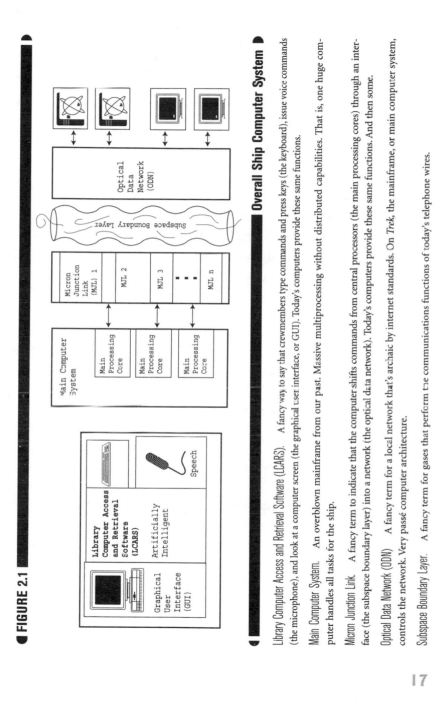

Overall Ship Computer System

Library Computer Access and Retrieval Software (LCARS).   A fancy way to say that crewmembers type commands and press keys (the keyboard), issue voice commands (the microphone), and look at a computer screen (the graphical user interface, or GUI). Today's computers provide these same functions.

Main Computer System.   An overblown mainframe from our past. Massive multiprocessing without distributed capabilities. That is, one huge computer handles all tasks for the ship.

Micron Junction Link.   A fancy term to indicate that the computer shifts commands from central processors (the main processing cores) through an interface (the subspace boundary layer) into a network (the optical data network). Today's computers provide these same functions. And then some.

Optical Data Network (ODN)   A fancy term for a local network that's archaic by internet standards. On *Trek*, the mainframe, or main computer system, controls the network. Very passé computer architecture.

Subspace Boundary Layer.   A fancy term for gases that perform the communications functions of today's telephone wires.

software); the main processing core; the micron junction links; the subspace boundary layer; and the optical data network (ODN). We'll briefly skate through the entire system and then examine each element in detail. According to the technical manual, the LCARS "provides both keyboard and verbal interface ability, incorporating highly sophisticated artificial intelligence routines and graphic display organization for maximum crew ease-of-use." This is a fancy way of saying that crewmembers type commands and press keys, issue voice commands (the verbal interface), and look at a computer screen. We have the equivalent of an LCARS today. Writing this chapter involved typing commands and pressing function keys. Voice recognition software can be bought over the counter at most computer stores. For a couple of months' wages you can buy a computer with 256 megabytes of random access memory (RAM) and dual Pentium processors, that with appropriate software will render three-dimensional moving images as quickly as the LCARS screen on *Star Trek*. In fact, a good modern screen has crisper colors and better image resolution.

As we type on our keyboard and gaze at the monitor in order, say, to write this book, the PC's two processors work together to handle our commands.* Just as all the processors in the main processing core of the *Enterprise* computer handle the commands that the crew supplies.

To back up this chapter (in case NT blows), we save it using another filename. We may backup the entire system on zip disks, CDs, or other media. The *Enterprise* computer, with its three main processing cores, is more like a giant IBM mainframe from the 1970s, with two mainframes providing total system backup—

---

*Not a great use of dual processors, but for now, we're keeping things simple. The dual processors come in handy during 3D graphics rendering.

in case one mainframe blows, the *Enterprise* crew has another ready to assume all system functions. The LCARS consoles are the equivalent of the 1970s graphic display terminals that connected to the old mainframes.

The micron junction links shift commands from the main processing cores through a subspace boundary layer into the ODN. Again, fancy terms for things we do today (though we don't do them at faster-than-light [FTL] speed). Let's suppose that this chapter is ready for our editor. Our transmission choices are: print the chapter and send it to the editor in an envelope, or e-mail the chapter to him. If we choose e-mail, the Internet does the trick. In our case, we dial a phone number and establish a modem connection to our Internet service provider. Over ordinary phone lines (or more high-speed lines, if someone has cash to burn), we transmit the chapter. The Internet service provider is our micron junction link. The telephone wires are our subspace boundary layer. Our ODN is the Internet. Somewhere in an indescribably messy editorial office, our editor logs onto the Internet and retrieves Chapter 2. Picture him sitting at his PC in our drawing of the *Enterprise* computer. He's over there on the right, looking at one of the terminals or control panels.

The most striking difference between the general design of our PC-linked Internet and the ODN setup of the *Enterprise* computer is that our technology is more advanced. Our version of the ODN—today's Internet—connects independent computers around the world. There's no mainframe controlling the Internet. On *Star Trek*, the ODN connects LCARS terminals to a giant mainframe that controls all system functions. This is a very old-fashioned networking design.

Now let's take a closer look at each part of the system and see if they are reasonable approximations of what our descendants will be using in a few hundred years.

The LCARS Interface

Suppose Lieutenant Commander Worf is glaring at the computer console screen on the main bridge. He's typing information into the main computer system while he issues a command to the computer to locate Captain Picard, whom he assumes is somewhere on the ship. (In fact, Picard has been spirited away by the mysterious superbeing Q, raising problems we'll discuss in a later chapter.)

The LCARS speech module picks up Worf's command. The *Technical Manual* describes the LCARS as an artificially-intelligent module that includes a graphical user interface. It doesn't tell us why the LCARS requires artificial intelligence. On the show itself, we see no indication of artificial intelligence in the LCARS. When addressing the computer, Worf says, "Computer, locate Captain Picard." He doesn't address the LCARS, nor does the LCARS respond. It's always the main computer system's voice that we hear.

As for the graphical-user interface, in our time it's a screen that displays text and pictures. But in the twenty-fourth century, the computer's interactions with users will be a good deal more advanced than this. The first question we need to ask is: If we're three hundred years into the future, why would Worf (or anyone) require a keyboard or any type of key-button control system? Won't keyboards have gone the way of the buggy whip?

It won't be all that long before invisible computers sense our presence in a room, cook our food, start our cars, do our laundry, design our clothing, and make it for us. Computers may even detect our emotional states and automatically know how to help us relax after a grueling day at work.

Our primary means of communicating with these computers will be the same one we use with each other: speech. By analyzing frequency and sound intensities, today's voice recognition software can recognize more than forty thousand English words. It does this by differentiating one phoneme from another.* However, to understand what someone is saying (as opposed to simply recognizing that someone has uttered the phoneme p rather than f), the software must be artificially intelligent. It's one thing for voice-recognition software to interpret a spoken command such as "Save file" or "Call Dr. Green's office." It's quite another for software to understand "What are the chances that Picard is still a human inside Locutus?" Phonemes alone don't suffice. Thus we assume the main computer system must be artificially intelligent. But this function is never performed by the LCARS on *Star Trek*.

Many prominent researchers think that tomorrow's computers will understand not only our voices but also our body language. Already, enormous research has been done in building computers that see and interpret our facial expressions. Since 1975, the Facial Action Coding System (FACS) has been used to create facial animations that portray human emotions. These systems interpret our expressions as belonging to a limited set of emotional states and respond in programmed ways. If the imaging software detects us smiling, for instance, the computer may play some of our favorite rock and roll. If it "sees" that we're nervous or impatient, it will forego the music and speed up its response time instead.

When it comes to facial recognition software, the LCARS is way behind today. And as for what's coming, the LCARS doesn't come close.

Here's a glimpse at where we think technology is heading. A doctor (who will be more like a bioengineer with a good bedside

---

* A phoneme is an individual speech sound, for example the "p" in "pat." Although the correspondence isn't exact, phonemes are, roughly speaking, the "atoms" of speech.

manner) injects micro or nanochips beneath your skin. McCoy and Crusher do this sort of thing with crewmembers all the time. In the real future, however, the computer chips inside your body will communicate wirelessly as a distributed network.

Sprain a muscle, and the nervous system tells your brain to feel pain. Touch something hot, and the nervous system tells your brain that your fingers are burning. Hear something loud, and the nervous system tells your brain that your ears hurt. In the future, the computer chips inside your body will detect such neurotransmissions as well as many other physical symptoms—for example, heart rate and cholesterol levels—and possibly release chemical antidotes. To state it simply, your body will be a network of microprocessors.

There's nothing to stop you from linking your body network into the future's version of the Internet, where everyone else's body is also linked. You can turn on the music chip in your toe, think "Bach's Fantasia in G Major" and hear it. If there's a new recording of it that you've just learned about, you can retrieve that rendition from across the globe, hear it, and never even activate your own music chip. You can transmit a work assignment to your boss by touching his hand (or kissing his feet . . . or blowing it to him). In fact, all you will need to do is sit and think, and your body network will do the rest.

This seems more like our future than Worf typing commands on a keyboard and staring at a computer screen. The LCARS seems more like a dumb terminal than an artificially intelligent workstation. Besides, the LCARS will be unnecessary, even as an intelligent front end to the ship's computer. At minimum, the main *Enterprise* computer—if indeed such a thing exists, which is unlikely—will sense Worf's presence on the bridge simply because his body network identifies him.

In addition, it's probably evident to you by now that Worf won't need to issue voice commands, either. He'll think, "Where is

Picard?" his body network will link to all the other body networks on the ship, and instantly, Picard's body network will respond.

If you think about where technology's heading, this makes perfect sense. Within a decade or two, we'll wave some fingers to indicate what we want our computers to do. The computer's sensors will visually identify our hand motions. Today's computers, even simple robots made with Lego* toys, use sensors to see.

Let's assume the following as givens: (1) the ship's computer recognizes and interprets the body networks—and the body language—of each individual, (2) the ship's computer includes wireless networks of individual processors, (3) these processors communicate with each other, with the "main" computer, and with every crewmember. It's our guess that possibly, in three or four hundred years, human speech may be unnecessary in many contexts.

In fact, if we make three more entirely plausible assumptions—that all the ship's instrumentation is controlled through virtual-reality simulations; that people interact with the computer strictly by gestures and whispered commands; and that personal communicators consist of subcutaneous implants in the crew's throats and ears—then we can imagine a truly bizarre scene. A person watching the bridge crew operate the ship would see only a group of people sitting in a bare room, apparently muttering to themselves while making random hand motions. This may indeed be the starship of the future, but it's lousy TV. That's why we need those keyboards, screen displays, and clearly spoken conversations. We twentieth-century viewers need visuals that we can instantly understand. To our descendants, the difference between

---

*The Lego company, in conjunction with MIT, introduced a Robotics Invention System in October of 1998. Children can now build fully functional robots equipped with sight, touch, temperature, and light sensors.

talking to a person and talking to a computer may be a distinction hardly worth noticing; but to us, it's very important indeed.

While we're talking about the LCARS, let's pause to think about Worf's communicator badge. If Worf isn't near an LCARS console, he may tap his badge and ask the computer to locate Captain Picard. How likely is this scenario?

It's predicted that within a few years, workers will wear tiny communicators equipped with infrared transmitters. These modern-day communicators will have the power of desktop PC's. They'll function like those in *Star Trek*, but they'll be even smaller. Prototypes have already been built and tested.

Today's communicators, as on *Star Trek*, let main-computer systems know where everyone is located. This is how lights turn on when Picard enters his quarters and how doors magically slide open for Captain Kirk. The future is now.

Why do crewmembers need to tap their badges to open a channel? Why not just issue a voice command to activate a communicator embedded beneath the skin of your throat? In the *Star Trek* future, a communicator may be so tiny that it'll be invisible and injected by a hyposspray beneath the skin.

In *The Next Generation* episode "Legacy," Data comments that he and Geordi can use a sensing device that "monitors bioelectric signatures of the crew in the event they get separated from the [escape] pod." This implies that, in the *Trek* universe, ordinary badge-tapping communicators are unnecessary. Even in the original series ("Patterns of Force"), Kirk instructs McCoy to "prepare a subcutaneous transponder in the event we can't use our communicators." McCoy then uses a hyposspray to inject the transponder.

And if injected nanocommunicators are already a part of *Star Trek*, why does Geordi need his visor to see? Surely, he'd have microscopic sensors implanted in his eyes. In "Future Imperfect"

(*TNG*), Geordi wears "cloned implants" rather than his visor. In the movie, *First Contact*, Geordi's eyes are totally cybernetic (and quite handsome). Whatever their form, Geordi's visual implants show that the problem of translating an electronic signal into a neural one has been solved—and if we can translate in one direction, we can do the reverse.

But let's return to the ship's computer, as described by the *Technical Manual*.

The LCARS polls every control panel on the ship at 30-millisecond intervals. All the control panels and terminals are hooked up to the ODN. These connections exist so the main processing core and/or quadritronic optical subprocessor (QOS) instantly knows all keyboard and speech commands issued on the ship.

First, it seems odd that the main processing core stores this information. The LCARS is defined as artificially intelligent. It should recognize and interpret voice commands as well as keystroke commands. In today's world, we don't need a huge mainframe computer to store and handle all our transmissions. We use the Internet, for example, and communicate directly from PC to PC. If Worf says "Where is Picard?" to his LCARS console, it should be able to query all the other LCARS consoles on the ship.

Supposedly, information travels between an LCARS console and the main processing core at FTL speed. Why is this necessary? Fingers don't type at FTL speed. People don't speak at FTL speed. Does the LCARS contain gigantic buffers to queue Worf's typed commands and spoken ideas, to store FTL-transmitted representations of entire galaxies for Worf to view on his screen? In today's world, electrons can course only so fast down circuits, no matter how close we jam the circuits together. That's why we're going to move from silicon circuitry to something else: maybe optical computers, maybe quantum computers, maybe some combination of approaches. So how does the LCARS screen keep up with the FTL-speed drawings and three-dimensional renderings? What kind of graphics cards are in those *Trek* consoles anyway?

Let's leave Worf and move to our second drawing, Figure 2.2, the main computer system.

◀ The Processor ▶

The *Technical Manual* tells us that the main computer system is "responsible in some way for the operation of virtually every other system of the vehicle." What does this mean?

To be blunt: The main computer system is a gigantic 1970s mainframe. Without it, nothing on the ship works. Even the way it's described—"The computer is directly analogous to the autonomic nervous system of a living being" and "The heart of the main computer system is a set of three redundant main processing cores"—reminds us of the way technical writers in the late 1970s described computers. By the mid-1980s, the use of "nervous system" and "heart" by technical writers was passé.

The CPU, or central processing unit, is called the computer's heart because it controls major system functions. Without a heart, you die. Without a CPU, the computer dies. The nervous system analogy refers to the networking, the cables, the wires, and the flow of electrons: just as in our bodies, signals move through the nerves by means of membrane potentials and neurotransmitters.

These analogies don't work very well any more. For one thing, our computer systems are more like a web of interconnected bodies and brains rather than a single being with a heart and a nervous system. A 1990s computer is tied to many different networks. Smaller local area networks (LANs) may feed directly onto larger company intranets, which may in turn tie directly into the global Internet. University networks hook to one another and also hook to the Internet. As do government agency networks. There is no central heart, no central nervous system.

We have no clue how the primary and upper levels shown in Figure 2.2 differ. The *Technical Manual* states only that each main processing core "comprises seven primary and three upper levels, each level containing an average of four modules." It appears that the main computer system of the *Enterprise* has an architecture much like a massive parallel-processing supercomputer.

According to the textbook, *Computer Architecture: A Quantitative Approach*[2] a processor is "the core of the computer and contains everything except the memory, input, and output. The processor is further divided into computation and control." Processing performance is often measured as clock cycles per instruction or clock cycle time, with the clock synchronizing propagation of signals throughout the computer. Processing speed is commonly defined as operations per second. In 1984, one of the authors thought it was cool to be part of a team that created a superminicomputer that processed ten million operations per second. Big deal. In June of 1997, Intel built a supercomputer that executed 1.34 trillion operations per second. This computer looked like the *Enterprise* mainframe. Engineers had to crawl through Jeffries tubes (or their Earth-based equivalent) to access 9,200 Pentium Pro processors in 86 system cabinets.

As seen in Figure 2.2, the main computer system of the *Enterprise* consists of:

(10 levels) * (4 processing modules per level) =
40 processing modules per main processing core

That's not even close to the 9,200 processors in the 1997 Intel supercomputer. But as we'll see, each *Trek* processing module contains hundreds of thousands of nanoprocessors.

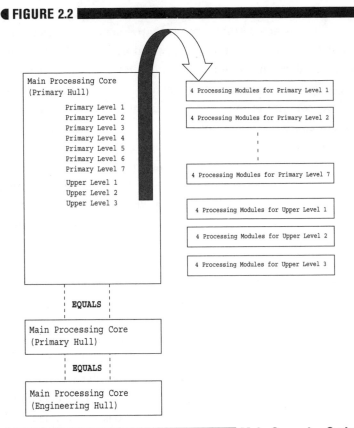

Main Processing Core (Primary Hull)		4 Processing Modules for Primary Level 1

Main Processing Core. The central computing unit of *Trek's* mainframe system. *Star Trek* doesn't define the functions of the primary and three upper levels. Supposedly, the second and third main processing cores are backups for the first. Everything runs at faster-than-light speed, implying that the main processing core may actually run backwards in time.

Processing Modules. A far-fetched fancy way to pretend that the computer has vast processing power. Each processing module supposedly contains hundreds of thousands of microscopic processors. They run in parallel—simultaneously handle multiple operations—at faster-than-light speed. Having signals running at 900,000 kilometers per second through microscopic circuits implies that information may arrive before it's sent.

Further, we're told that each of the three main processing cores is redundant—that is, they run in "parallel clock-sync with each other, providing 100% redundancy." And that they do this at rates "significantly higher than the speed of light." What could this statement possibly mean? It's one thing to say that data is transmitted at lightspeed. But it makes no sense to say that clock cycles per instruction run at lightspeed or that the clock cycle time is significantly higher than lightspeed. This is the same as claiming that a clock runs at 900,000 kilometers per second. Clocks don't run in kilometers, millimeters, or any other spatial unit. Machine speed is measured in operations per second, not in kilometers per second.

On the other hand, we can make the very vague statement that the faster a signal travels during a finite amount of time, the more operations the machine processes per second. If each signal represents one operation, and signals suddenly travel more quickly, then okay, the computer might process more instructions per time unit. But remember that Moore's Law (in one of its versions) says that computer speed doubles every 18 months. If we took an optical computer (where signals travel, say, at lightspeed) and replaced all its circuitry with FTL circuitry (where signals travel three times as fast), we might triple our computer's processing speed. Under Moore's Law, that's a gain of just over two years.

And having signals travel 900,000 kilometers per second adds very little speed if the circuit is microscopic. And wouldn't the system clock run backwards? Wouldn't information arrive before it was sent?—and so get sent back again in an endless sequence?

And . . .

As McCoy might say, "Damn it, Jim, we're computer scientists, not physicists!"

Let's continue our journey through the *Technical Manual*. The manual states that if one of the main processing cores in the primary hull fails, then the other assumes the total primary computing load for the ship without interruption. Also that the main processing core in the engineering hull is a backup, in case the two primary units fail. So . . . why do the holodeck simulations get interrupted in so many episodes? Why do the food replicators constantly go haywire? In *The Next Generation* episode "Cost of Living," two hundred replicators break down.* Are all three main processing cores down? If so, how is *anything* running?

Perhaps if we look more closely at the main processing core itself (Figure 2.3), as described in the manual, we'll come up with an answer.

Each main processing core is made up of a series of miniature subspace field generators (MSFG). These create a symmetrical (nonpropulsive) field distortion of 3350 millicochranes within the FTL core elements. According to the manual, "This permits transmission and processing of optical data within the core at rates significantly higher than lightspeed."[3]

Further, we're told that a nanocochrane is a measure of subspace field stress and is equal to one billionth of a cochrane. These definitions are about warp speed. A cochrane is the amount of field stress needed to generate a speed of c, the speed of light. One cochrane = c, 2 cochranes = 2c, and so on.

Warp factor 1 = 1 cochrane
Warp factor 2 = 10 cochranes
Warp factor 3 = 39 cochranes

---

*To isolate the problems, Geordi and Data crawl through a Jeffries tube and use a device resembling an old AM radio with blinking lights, plus a miniscreen. But even more fun is the movie, *Star Trek VI: The Undiscovered Country*, in which the ship has a huge kitchen complete with dozens of cooks, all making turkeys, biscuits, and mashed potatoes. *Using pots and pans!* Where are the replicators?

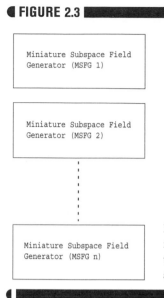

Each main processing core is made up of many miniature subspace field generators that allow internal processing of data to run significantly faster than lightspeed.

◀ ██████████████████████████████████ Main Processing Core ▶

There's even a chart in the *Technical Manual* that shows "velocity in multiples of lightspeed" on the y-axis and "warp factor" on the x-axis, with "power usage in megajoules/cochrane" and "power usage approaches infinity" designated. We're told that warp 10 is impossible because at warp 10, speed would be "infinite." (Never mind that the original series' ship sometimes exceeds warp 10. In "The Changeling" (*TOS*), the *Enterprise* hits warp 11.)

So 3350 millicochranes = 3.35 cochranes = warp factor slightly above warp 1 (because 10 cochranes = warp factor 2). The implication is that the MSFGs allow internal processing of data within each main processing core to run significantly faster than lightspeed. Sorry, dear readers. Even if it meant something to say that a computer's processing speed is faster than light, this is still implausible. Just because FTL travel is possible for starships, that doesn't imply that machinery within an FTL field will operate at such speeds.

A Twenty-Fourth-Century Mainframe

FTL signal transmission presumably affects redundancy, since the three cores transfer information from one to another at warp velocity. Anyone accessing one of the three computer cores would find the exact same data on each. Feeding information into one core is the same as feeding it into all three. This scenario is hard to believe. In emergency situations, if either of the main processing cores in the primary hull fails, the other would assume total primary computing load for the ship without interruption. As would the processing core in the engineering hull used for backup. The information in each would be exactly the same. In other words, the linked computers would achieve 100 percent redundancy. But only if we accept the notion that they can "operate at FTL speeds."

If we don't, then it's impossible for the three computer cores to be 100 percent redundant. Though the machines might operate extremely fast, information transfer would still take nanoseconds or microseconds to complete. Not much time to us. But as we'll discuss in the chapter on navigation and battle, the delay might prove crucial to a starship.

◀ Core Elements ▶

The main processing cores consist of individual processors, called core elements, that actually do the computing—running programs, interpreting and carrying out instructions, calculating addresses in memory, and so on. According to the manual, "core elements are based on FTL nanoprocessor units arranged into optical transtator clusters of 1,024 segments. In turn, clusters are grouped into processing modules composed of 256 clusters controlled by a bank of sixteen isolinear chips."[4]

Let's try to translate this into English. Taking what we know about the ship's computer and combining it with the above description, we come up with Figure 2.4.

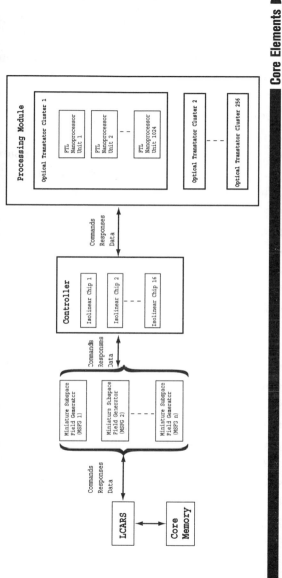

A vast array of faster-than-light-speed microscopic nanoprocessor units that do the actual computing. Each processing module has 256 groups—optical transtator clusters—of 1,024 FTL nanoprocessor units.

Since the *Star Trek* technical manual devotes just two sentences to core elements, we have to guess what an FTL nanoprocessor is, what an optical transtator cluster is, what the segments are, and what the sixteen isolinear chips do. This drawing shows the LCARS communicating with what we may call the controller through the miniature subspace field generators. The controller is the bank of sixteen isolinear chips. These chips may constitute a front-end parallel processing unit that interprets and consolidates commands and responses, and perhaps buffers data for faster transmission.

Since the manual devotes just two sentences to core elements, we have to guess what an FTL nanoprocessor is, what an optical transtator cluster is, what the segments are, and what the sixteen isolinear chips do. Figure 2.4 shows the LCARS communicating with what we may call the controller through the miniature subspace field generators. The controller is the bank of sixteen isolinear chips. These chips may constitute a front-end parallel processing unit that interprets and consolidates commands and responses, and perhaps buffers data for faster transmission. (Though how data buffers can speed up transmission that's already going faster than light is beyond our comprehension.) Again, it looks as if the architecture of the *Enterprise* computer is a mishmash of mainframe architecture, supercomputer architecture, and a fantasy of FTL circuitry coursing through gigantic metal machinery.

Let's continue with the transmission of commands, responses, and data from the controller to and from the processing modules. We're told that each processing module has 256 optical transtator clusters, each containing 1,024 FTL nanoprocessor units.

Multiplying these numbers together, we deduce that each *Enterprise* processing module has 262,144 FTL nanoprocessor units. Remember that the ship has 40 processing modules per main processing core (see Figure 2.2) and that it has three main processing cores, for a total of 120 processing modules. Onboard the entire ship, therefore, we have 262,144 * 120 = 31,457,280 FTL nanoprocessor units.

That's a lot of processing power! Thirty-one million nanoprocessors certainly beats the 9,200 processors of Intel's 1997 supercomputer.

What's a Nanoprocessor?

Today we use microprocessors, built from microtechnology. We measure parts in micrometers, or millionths of a meter. And small as they are, microprocessors are at least big enough to see.

Today's computer scientists are forging into a new area, called nanotechnology. Nanoprocessors imply measurement in the billionths of a meter. In other words, molecular-based circuitry: invisible computers, and extremely fast.

Star Trek gives us little information about the 31,457,280 nanoprocessors that are the ship's computer. This is material we'd love to see on future episodes. If the processors are microscopic, why does Geordi crawl through Jeffries tubes and use what appears to be a laser soldering gun to fix computer components? Why not a pair of wire cutters and some needlenose pliers? In short, why is manual tweaking necessary? A computer system this sophisticated should fix itself. A main thrust of nanotechnology is that the microscopic components operate as tiny factories. They repair themselves, build new components, and learn through artificial intelligence. They are much like the nanites in the episode "Evolution" (*TNG*). Speaking of which, it's most peculiar that people using nanotechnology computers would be so shocked by the discovery of the nanites.

Even Data's manual adjustments are pretty silly (though a lot of fun to watch). For example, in "The Schizoid Man" (*TNG*), Geordi checks Data's programming with a device that looks like a toaster. Certainly an android with self diagnostics and self repair, with a fully redundant and highly complex positronic neural net—well, such an android would not require a huge toaster-like device as a repair tool!

Also, how does Worf (in "A Fistful of Datas," *TNG*) rig up wires between a communicator and a personal weapons shield? Is it possible to connect wires from something that's invisible to a wireless communicator using a molecular-sized energy source?

◀ Memory ████████████████████████████████ ▶

At the end of the twentieth century, memory comes in several varieties. RAM, which can be accessed at the byte level, contains instructions and data used by the processors. Flash RAM also contains instructions and data but is read and written in blocks rather than bytes. Storing files, such as this chapter, is done using disk drives, floppies, zip disks, CDs, and tapes.

The core memory consists of isolinear optical storage chips, which *Trek* defines as nanotech devices. Under the heading "Core Memory," the *Technical Manual* says that "Memory storage for main core usage is provided by 2,048 dedicated modules of 144 isolinear optical storage chips. . . . Total storage capacity of each module is about 630,000 kiloquads, depending on software configuration."[5] Figure 2.5 shows how we see core memory.

Oddly enough, no one on *Star Trek* ever mentions disk space, which is where files are actually stored. If core memory really means disk space and not RAM, then where's the RAM? The manual explicitly references "memory access" to and from the LCARS when discussing kiloquads. In today's world of computers, memory buses do "memory access" to memory chips, or RAM, not to hard drives.

The same manual defines the isolinear optical chips as the "primary software and data storage medium." This phrase implies hard drive space. But then, in the next sentence, the manual refers to how the chips represent many advances over the earlier "crystal memory cards." This sentence implies RAM. Because *Trek* people use the isolinear optical chips in tricorders and personal access display devices (PADDs) for "information transport," it

A Twenty-Fourth-Century Mainframe

36

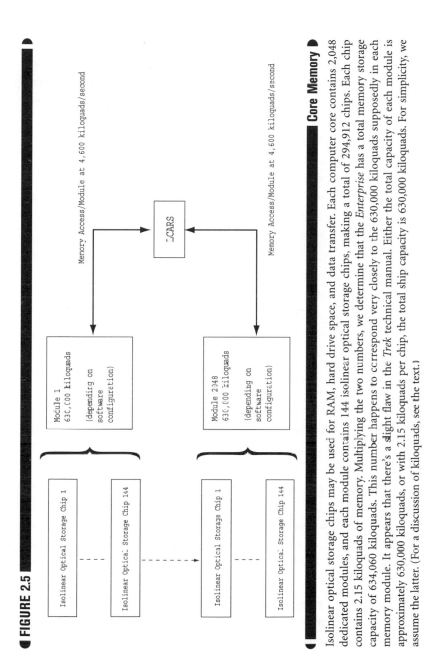

FIGURE 2.5

Isolinear Optical Storage Chip 1 ... **Isolinear Optical Storage Chip 144**

Module 1
630,000 kiloquads

(depending on
software
configuration)

Memory Access/Module at 4,600 kiloquads/second

LCARS

Isolinear Optical Storage Chip 1 ... **Isolinear Optical Storage Chip 144**

Module 2048
630,000 kiloquads

(depending on
software
configuration)

Memory Access/Module at 4,600 kiloquads/second

Core Memory

Isolinear optical storage chips may be used for RAM, hard drive space, and data transfer. Each computer core contains 2,048 dedicated modules, and each module contains 144 isolinear optical storage chips, making a total of 294,912 chips. Each chip contains 2.15 kiloquads of memory. Multiplying the two numbers, we determine that the *Enterprise* has a total memory storage capacity of 634,060 kiloquads. This number happens to correspond very closely to the 630,000 kiloquads supposedly in each memory module. It appears that there's a slight flaw in the *Trek* technical manual. Either the total capacity of each module is approximately 630,000 kiloquads, or with 2.15 kiloquads per chip, the total ship capacity is 630,000 kiloquads. For simplicity, we assume the latter. (For a discussion of kiloquads, see the text.)

37

sounds as if the chips are the future version of today's floppy disks, zip disks, or CDs. A footnote in the *Technical Manual* states that the isolinear optical chips reflect "the original 'microtape' data cartridges used in the original series." Which also implies that the chips are descendants of floppies or zips or Jazz disks.

Sorting through the technobabble, we're forced to conclude that isolinear optical chips are used for RAM (the references to core memory), hard drive space, *and* data transfer (the references to floppies, the PADDs, etc). If pushed, we shrug and say that isolinear optical chips are used for everything. Each chip is a nanoprocessor with associated memory, and each chip also serves as a disk drive. Of course, each chip includes all required input/output and memory buses. Sure. And LaForge and O'Brien crawl through a Jeffries tube with socket wrenches whenever one of these chips needs fixing.

Our future will be with invisible nanotech computers. These computers will incorporate processing functions, memory, and storage space. They may do everything, just as the isolinear chips supposedly do everything. But in reality, our chips will be interconnected in a widely distributed network of processors and storage media. There will be no need to store massive amounts of information in any one location.

Each computer core contains 2,048 dedicated modules, and each module contains 144 isolinear optical storage chips, making a total of 294,912 chips. Each chip contains 2.15 kiloquads of memory in standard holographic format, according to the *Technical Manual*. Multiplying our two numbers together, we determine that the *Enterprise* has a total memory storage capacity of 634,060 kiloquads. This number happens to correspond very closely to the 630,000 kiloquads supposedly in each memory module.

At this point, it appears that there's a slight flaw in the manual. Either the total capacity of each module is approximately 630,000 kiloquads,* or with 2.15 kiloquads per chip, the total ship capacity is 630,000 kiloquads. For simplicity, let's assume the latter.

So what's a kiloquad? We don't know. The designers of *Star Trek* dare not jump on a limb and try to define it. According to the *Star Trek Encyclopedia*, "No, we don't know how many bytes are in a kiloquad. We don't even want to know. The reason the term was invented was specifically to avoid describing the data capacity of *Star Trek*'s computers in 20th century terms."[6]

The series' writers feared defining the kiloquad too closely for obvious reasons: people might calculate whether the ship's computers were adequate to do all the fantastic things the writers were making them do. However, that hasn't stopped *Star Trek* fans from trying to figure out the size of a kiloquad, and being fans ourselves, we'll play the same game.

With kilo defined as one thousand, the meaningful part of the term is quad. Checking a dictionary reveals that the only numerical term involving quad is quadrillion, which is defined as a thousand trillion (10^{15}). Thus, it's easy enough to deduce (as have many other Trekkers) that a kiloquad equals 1,000 quadrillion bytes. Breaking it down further, a kiloquad's the same as a million trillion bytes (10^{18} bytes).

As first seen in the original series episode "The Naked Now," isolinear optical chips are approximately the size of a 3.5-inch floppy disk. We'll use that standard for our model. In the *Star Trek* universe, an isolinear optical storage chip, approximately the size of a 3.5-inch floppy disk, contains 2.15 kiloquads of memory, which we assume to be 2.15×10^{18} bytes. These kiloquads are in "standard holographic format." Is this plausible?

---

* This also implies that each chip supplies 4,375 kiloquads of memory (630,000 kiloquads per module) / (144 chips/module).

As we mentioned in the first chapter, many computer scientists predict that holographic storage units will be the memory units of the future. Lambertus Hesselink of Stanford University believes that a cube a centimeter on a side eventually may store a terabyte of data (10^{12} bytes).[7]

Keeping in mind that a floppy disk doesn't have a depth of one centimeter, we can still approximate the amount of holographic storage contained on our kiloquad floppy disk.

First, suppose that Hesselink is correct. Suppose also that future scientists will do a bit better than Hesselink's prediction and will store a terabyte in a volume of 1 by 1 by ¼ centimeter.

Recalling that one inch equals 2.54 centimeters, we quickly determine that 3.5 inches yields 8.89 centimeters. If we store a terabyte of data in 1 by 1 by ¼ centimeter, then we end up with something like the holographic floppy disk in Figure 2.6.

But 81×10^{12} bytes per chip is not even close to 2.15 kiloquads, which is 2.15×10^{18} bytes. On the other hand, if scientists predict today that we'll store a terabyte in a cubic centimeter, then perhaps within three or four hundred years, we'll store 2.15 kiloquads in "standard holographic format." It seems possible. Further, it's quite possible that the *Enterprise* has a total of 634,060 kiloquads of memory and/or storage capacity.

That's a *lot* of memory. Which is why the writers of *Star Trek* are astute in not assigning a value to a kiloquad!

Which leads us to ask if so much memory is necessary.

In "Wolf in the Fold" (*TOS*), Captain Kirk has the ship's computer search for crimes similar to those Mr. Scott is accused of committing. He also asks the computer to search for certain keywords like "Redjack." In both cases, the computer finds matches on other worlds over a period of centuries. This implies that the computer contains a vast amount of information about life on Federation planets over the centuries.

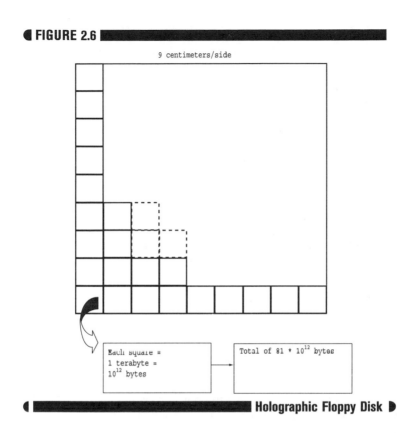

9 centimeters/side

Each square =
1 terabyte =
10^{12} bytes

Total of $81 * 10^{12}$ bytes

▬▬▬▬▬▬▬▬▬▬▬▬▬▬▬▬▬▬▬ **Holographic Floppy Disk** ▶

In "The Neutral Zone" (*TNG*), Clair Raymond searches for her descendants using the computer. Not only does she find her family tree, but she locates information about her grandson many times removed, his photo, and where he lives. Leading us to believe that the ship's computer maintains extensive files about every citizen in the Federation.

In "Eye of the Needle" (*VGR*), the crew of *Voyager* contacts a Romulan science vessel through a wormhole that cuts through both space and time. They tell their plight to a Romulan scientist, Telek R'Mor. He promises to send a chip containing information

A Twenty-Fourth-Century Mainframe

about *Voyager* to the Federation in 2371. But *Voyager's* computer reveals that Telek R'Mor died before the delivery date. Implying that information about Romulans is also available in the ship's memory banks.

Throughout all the *Next Generation, Deep Space Nine,* and *Voyager* adventures, the main computer is used to access famous plays, music, and books composed over the centuries. Extensive medical data on all known species belonging to the Federation is stored in the core memory. Thousands of battles fought by Federation starships are kept on file as reference, as are records of the adventures of other starships. As noted in "Legacy" (*TNG*), the computer stores every crewmember's complete DNA pattern. The computer seems to contain all knowledge and records compiled by the Federation. Is this possible, even with 630,000—or 1,290,240,000—kiloquads of memory?

Futurist Michael Dertouzos describes information in terms of units called LOCs.[8] One LOC is all the data contained in the United States Library of Congress. If we count only words, not pictures, films, or sound recordings, Dertouzos estimates this to be 100 terabytes (100×10^{12} bytes). Making one LOC equal to 10^{14} bytes.

Dertouzos estimates that all the information in the world, including all movies, sound recordings, individual data files, government files, corporate databases and so on, is approximately 10,000 LOCs, or 10^{18} bytes. This is the same as one kiloquad. Quite a coincidence.

Jumping three hundred years into the future, we're informed that the Federation consists of approximately 150 star systems (*First Contact*), with a population of less than one trillion beings ("The Last Outpost," *TNG*, and other episodes). Assuming that a number of those star systems have more than one inhabited planet, there might be 250 total worlds in the Federation, with approximately four billion people per world.

Many of those worlds have much smaller populations. Moreover, many of them began as, or still are, colonies of various space-going races. Still, even if we assume that every planet in the Federation has the same history and population of today's Earth, the total knowledge of those worlds would be 250 kiloquads. Now, since three hundred years have passed and interstellar exploration has added huge amounts of information to our knowledge of the universe, let's multiply that information by 1,000. Giving us a universal library of 1,000 * 250 kiloquads (which is the same as 2.5×10^{23} bytes).

Each isolinear optical storage chip contains 2.15 kiloquads. Now, 250 kiloquads divided by 2.15 kiloquads per chip yields 116 chips. And then, multiplying by 1,000, we get a total of 116,000 chips required to store the universal library. Fortunately, each redundant computer core of the *Enterprise* contains over 290,000 chips, a more than ample amount.

Of course, if the ship's computer is in constant contact with other Federation computers, there would be no need to store all information in the known universe. In our world today, someone wanting a dose of Brazilian music need only hop onto the Internet, search for Brazilian music, and launch an audio player. There's no need to store Brazilian music on your PC. Why can't people do this sort of thing on *Star Trek*? If Picard can talk to another starship captain with realtime visual and audio clarity, why can't he listen to a concerto that's stored on another starship?

We need to mention that in the *Voyager* episode "Twisted," the ship contacts a strange being that exists as a spacial distortion. After some unusual plot turns, the creature exchanges information with the ship's library. We're told that the entity has written twenty million gigaquads of information into the ship's computer.

Here we go again. What the heck is a gigaquad? And how much information is in twenty million of them? Does this episode make sense?

First, giga means 10^9, and we remember that a quad is a quadrillion, 10^{15} bytes. So one gigaquad is $10^9 \times 10^{15}$ bytes, or 10^{24} bytes. Twenty-million gigaquads means that we have $(2 * 10^7)(10^{24}$ bytes). We're in the neighborhood of 2×10^{31} bytes of information. That's more than the 2.5×10^{23} bytes available in the ship's library. Remember that 116,000 of the available 290,000 chips are used to store the ship's library. But even if we store two entire libraries in 232,000 chips, the *Voyager* computer wouldn't come close to having $2 * 10^{31}$ bytes of information. There's no way that the entity can write to more storage space than *Voyager* has. It would take roughly ten million *Voyagers* to store twenty-million gigaquads.

Since we're discussing information, we ought to mention that despite a communications system that somehow works instantly between star systems (impossible by all known physical laws, even on *Star Trek*) it's still inconceivable to expect the database and memory files of one starship to be redundant—that is, exactly identical and always up to date—with that of another ship. Or with all the ships in Starfleet.

Let's assume the *Enterprise* is in constant communication with Starfleet headquarters, and that all information recorded on the ship's computer—including every log entry, every medical note made by Dr. Crusher, every promotion, every new species encountered, every new planet surveyed—is instantly transmitted to the computers at headquarters. Before this information can be sent to other starships (assuming they too are in constant instantaneous contact with Starfleet command), it must be sorted, studied, and processed by Starfleet personnel. Otherwise, on every Federation starship, we'd have a duplicate Dr. Moriarty trying to take over from the holodeck ("Ship in a Bottle," *TNG*).

It's evident from a number of episodes that this constant exchange of information doesn't take place. Otherwise, Data's experiment with Lal ("The Offspring," *TNG*) would never occur.

Nor would the crew be able to promise the Paxans that their existence would be kept secret ("Clues," *TNG*). It's most likely that at specific intervals, a subspace transmission of data is sent from Federation starships to fleet headquarters. And that similar transmissions are made from headquarters to all ships, updating computer records and databases.

◀ Distributed Processing Network ███ ▶

The final component of the *Enterprise's* computer system is the distributed processing network (DPN). This is supposedly a network of "dedicated optical links" distributed all over the ship "to augment the main cores." The DPN does not use the FTL core elements. It "improves overall system response" and also provides redundancy for emergency situations.

Each quadritronic optical subprocessor (QOS) accesses from one to three main processing cores via a dedicated optical link (as shown in Figure 2.7). The technical manual doesn't explain anything about the QOS nor the overall DPN architecture.

Frankly, neither the QOS nor DPN makes sense.

The manual states that if the main computer system crashes, some QOS/DPN backup mechanism keeps the ship running. Let's assume that the main computer system does crash. It happens to fuel the optical data network—that is, without the main computer system, the ODN crashes, too. This architecture offers no redundancy for emergency situations. The manual states that the quadritronic optical subprocessors are part of the optical data network. If the ODN dies, then all the quadritronic optical subprocessors die. Who cares if there are dedicated optical links from each QOS to the main computer? The whole system is down.

And if the main processing cores are all dead, perhaps the LCARS is dead as well.

FIGURE 2.7

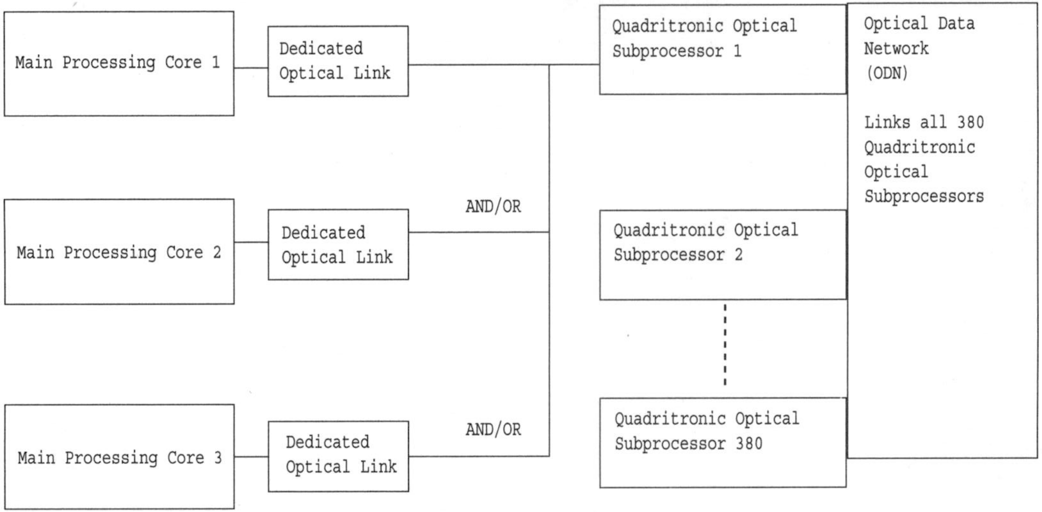

```
Main Processing Core 1 ── Dedicated Optical Link ── Quadritronic Optical Subprocessor 1 ── Optical Data Network (ODN)

                                                                                            Links all 380
                                                                                            Quadritronic
                                                                                            Optical
                                                                                            Subprocessors

                              AND/OR

Main Processing Core 2 ── Dedicated Optical Link ── Quadritronic Optical Subprocessor 2

                                                    - - - - - -

                              AND/OR

Main Processing Core 3 ── Dedicated Optical Link ── Quadritronic Optical Subprocessor 380
```

Distributed Processing Network (DPN)

Each quadritronic optical subprocessor accesses from one to three main processing cores via a dedicated optical link. The optical data network (ODN) links all 380 quadritronic optical subprocessors. The DPN includes the main processors, optical links, processors, and networking components. We're told that, if the main computer system crashes, some QOS/DPN mechanism keeps the ship running. Unfortunately, neither the QOS nor DPN makes sense.

Further, if the DPN isn't running at FTL, for whatever that's worth, how does it "improve overall system response"?

To determine if any of this makes sense, we'll merge Figure 2.1 with Figure 2.7. The result is Figure 2.8.

The LCARS is hooked directly to the main computer system and the dedicated optical links. The dedicated optical links, in turn, hook directly to the ODN. If the main computer system crashes, the ODN crashes. (Face it, folks: if the system dies, there's nothing left to run the network. Where's the operating system? In the main computer.) There is no point to the dedicated optical links. If the main computer system and the ODN crash, then the optical links also die. The LCARS may function as standalone processors, providing some small amount of backup data. Neither the technical manual nor the actual TV shows indicate that this occurs.

We see no point to the DPN. It is illogical.

◀ Personal Access Display Devices ▦▦ ▶

In chapter 1 we discussed communicators and what appear to be laptop computers on *TNG*, *VGR*, and *DS9*. We'll close with a brief look at PADDs.

In the original series, PADDs were the size of clipboards and appeared to serve a similar purpose. Their resemblance to portable computers was minimal. In *The Next Generation*, PADDs had shrunk in size and gained in power to become handheld computers directly linked to the ship's computer. A PADD serves not only as a personal computer but also as a communication device and even a lock-on node from the starship's transporter. According to the *Technical Manual*, a PADD has a dimension of 10 × 15 × 1 centimeter and a total memory capacity of 4.3 kiloquads (that is, 4.3 times the total information now stored on Earth). In theory, a

◀ FIGURE 2.8

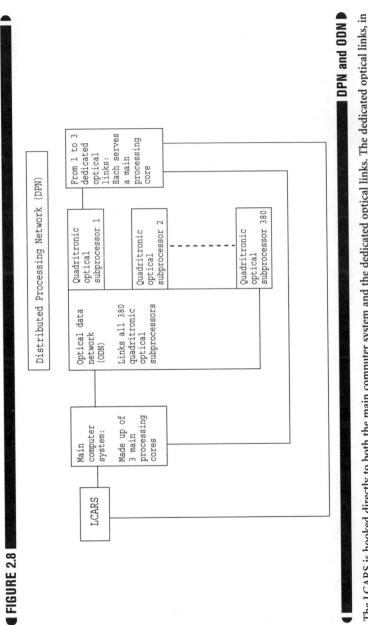

Distributed Processing Network (DPN)

LCARS

Main computer system:

Made up of 3 main processing cores

Optical data network (ODN)

Links all 380 quadritronic optical subprocessors

Quadritronic optical subprocessor 1

Quadritronic optical subprocessor 2

Quadritronic optical subprocessor 380

From 1 to 3 dedicated optical links:
Each serves a main processing core

DPN and ODN ▶

The LCARS is hooked directly to both the main computer system and the dedicated optical links. The dedicated optical links, in turn, hook directly to the optical data network. If the main computer system crashes, the ODN crashes. The architecture offers no remedy for computer crashes.

crewmember using a PADD with the proper access codes could navigate the starship from his quarters.

Again we find science overtaking science fiction. The past few years have seen the rise of handheld computers only slightly bigger than a PADD and with many of the same features. These devices continue to shrink, and computers the size of watches are already available. Life imitates art, then surpasses it. Why carry around a PADD when molecular implants will allow you to converse with invisible computers in the wall? It's in the future, and not three hundred years from now.

◀ Yesterday's Technology, and Tomorrow's ▶

Our tour of the *Star Trek* computer has shown us an architecture that is already several decades old. The *Enterprise* computer in the original series is a 1960s computer blown up to gigantic speed and power. The computers of *The Next Generation*, *Voyager*, and *Deep Space Nine* are configurations from the 1970s and 1980s blown up to gigantic speed and power. None of these computers even reflect today's technical realities, much less what we expect tomorrow. Here are some aspects we expect will be quite different.

◀ Size ▶

Our computers are not getting bigger, they're shrinking. If you need to fix circuits in your PC, a wrench and a screwdriver won't get you very far. You can't fix your processor chip's circuitry with tools from your garage. The isolinear optical storage chip is too big, as well. Today's microprocessor chip is the size of a sugar packet. There's no way that a nanoprocessor chip of the future will be the size of a floppy disk.

◀ Mainframe Configuration ██████████████ ▶

There are still computer systems in use today that have configurations like the main computer of *Star Trek*. An old IBM mainframe or a VAX superminicomputer sitting in a cold room, with display terminals networked to it. But these are old systems. Far more prevalent are increasingly powerful PCs distributed around the globe and linked by the Internet. Everyone has local processing power. Nobody relies on a mainframe down at headquarters to prepare his monthly expense report. *Star Trek* computers have yet to reflect the technology of the 1990s.

◀ Extremely Fast Processors ██████████████ ▶

Processing speed today continues to escalate. In noting increasing processing speeds, as well as today's research into optical and holographic technology, *Star Trek* does acknowledge some real computer trends. Sadly, though, it pushes these trends into exaggerated and sometimes meaningless fantasy.

◀ Centralized Storage and Processing ████████ ▶

Information today is distributed on PCs all over the world and linked by means of the Internet. The trend is clearly away from centralized data warehouses toward distributed information storage and processing. No computer today stores all information in the known universe. One of the marvels of the 1990s was Intel's supercomputer with 9,200 processors cranking 1.34 trillion operations per second. Still, such machines are uncommon to say the least. *Star Trek* reflects trends from an earlier time, the 1970s and 1980s.

What do we expect from real computers in the time of *Star Trek*? Remember, we're talking about computers in three to four hundred years. They'll be nothing like the computers of the 1960s, 70s, or 80s. Nor like anything we have today.

Rather, they'll be invisible. They'll be in our walls, our air, our clothing, ourselves. Our bodies will merge flesh and computer technology. This is commonly called nanotechnology. Microscopic computers will dissolve our blood clots, heal our wounds, prolong our age, cure our diseases. Being artificially intelligent, the computers inside our bodies will retrieve information based on our changing interests and needs, draw conclusions for us, write and transmit our reports, help us become better artists, musicians, thinkers. These computers will repair themselves and will communicate with one another, just as computers communicate with each other today. Your body will contain a distributed processing network of microscopic computers. Your body network will communicate with mine.

Each computer will access information and routines stored in any computer anywhere in the known universe. A computer in your body network will obtain a symphony, play, book, personnel file of an employee, DNA patterns of your child, police records of a suspect—literally anything that you're authorized to access—from any computer anywhere. No more keyboards. No more voice recognition. Your DNA pattern or a combination of other unique biological stamps will serve as your password. You will think, "Where is Picard?" and your body network will find his body network, even if he's on another starship in a distant galaxy.

Around us, microscopic robots will fix the structures in which we live and play, mend our clothes, repair our equipment and roads, and manicure the grass. We'll live in a world of science fiction, except it'll be everyday stuff to us.

Given sensor capabilities, self maintenance and repair, and artificial intelligence, a real starship of the twenty-fourth century may come so close to being alive and sentient that the difference is more philosophical than practical (as in "Tin Man," *TNG*).

Star Trek cannot show us what the future really will be like. If it tried to portray future computer technology more accurately, *Trek* would fail as a television program. The characters would sit and groan, and rarely move. The threats from aliens would be microscopic and thwarted before a character could part his lips. To be good television—with action, adventure, and plot—*Trek* needs visual stimuli and entities, alien threats that are not so easily thwarted, and characters that run, scream, pull computer cables from the ceilings, and fix the ship with wrenches in the nick of time. But when we ask if *Star Trek* is an accurate depiction of what the future holds, we have to answer: Not even close.

Security

In the twenty-fourth century, hunger, disease, and poverty no longer exist within the Federation. Nor do racism or sexism or any other type of discrimination. Most people appear to be happy. Crimes of violence have been largely eliminated from daily life, leading to a more trusting and open society. Robbery and theft make little sense in a time of unlimited abundance.

A world without criminals needs little law enforcement. Which unfortunately suggests that the few illegal acts that do occur often go unpunished. For example, we note the following incidents from the original series:

- Kodos the Executioner, one-time planetary governor of Tarsus IV who responsible for the deaths of hundreds of civilians, remains at large under an assumed identity, that of the actor, Anton Karidian, for twenty years. ("The Conscience of the King," *TOS*)
- Mr. Scott is accused of several brutal killings on the planet Argelius II. Though Scott's prosecutor knows way too much about the crimes, no one

suspects the officer of any wrongdoing. ("Wolf in the Fold," *TOS*)

- Captain Garth, a famous Federation Starfleet captain who has gone insane, seizes control of the penal colony on the planet Elba II. ("Whom Gods Destroy," *TOS*)
- The Federation starship, *Aurora*, is stolen by scientist, Dr. Sevrin, and his followers, to hunt for a mythical planet they believe is Eden. ("The Way to Eden," *TOS*)

If we jump forward to the time of Picard, Sisko, and Janeway, there's no appreciable change in crime-fighting techniques or security measures. We note the following crimes, among many:

- An extragalactic intelligence gains control over important Starfleet officers. Only after a number of extremely unusual policy decisions and shifts in key personnel is the intruder detected. ("Conspiracy," *TNG*)
- Crewman First Class Simon Tarses becomes a member of Starfleet (and gets to serve on the *Enterprise*) by falsifying his admission application to conceal that his grandfather is a Romulan. This information isn't discovered until Tarses is accused of sabotage during an investigation on the *Enterprise*. ("The Drumhead," *TNG*)
- The Red Squad, a group of Starfleet cadets, sabotage Earth's power grid, with the blame for the incident falling on alien shapeshifters. Again, only through coincidence are the true culprits revealed ("Homefront," *DS9*).

- Dr. Julian Bashir's parents, realizing their young son, Julian, is mentally handicapped, take him off-world to an illegal clinic where his DNA patterns are enhanced, greatly augmenting his intelligence and coordination. The operation is not discovered until years later, and only then through happenstance. ("Dr. Bashir, I Presume?" *DS9*)

Some of these episodes rank among *Star Trek's* finest adventures. Yet, from a strictly logical point of view, these incidents are unbelievable based on the technology of the time. In every instance, the crime was discovered not through investigation but by chance. Worse, most of these incidents involve Starfleet officers, which indicates a shocking lack of internal security in an organization charged with protecting the safety of the Federation.[*]

Life in the twenty-third and twenty-fourth centuries is obviously much different from today. Clearly, personal freedoms are strictly protected by the government and any attempt to infringe on them ("Paradise Lost," *DS9*) is regarded with suspicion. Still, considering the power and scope of Federation computer systems, the lack of effective security in the *Star Trek* universe is perhaps the most unbelievable aspect of the shows.

It's quite clear why security is so lax. If it wasn't, dozens of episodes would disappear from the ships' logs. Believable security is the bane of all script writers (and most novelists). It stretches

---

[*]Actually, these security problems are just one system of a general ineptitude. Considering how many times landing parties are infected by exotic diseases that they then bring back to the *Enterprise*, it's amazing the crew has survived at all. No more astonishing than the fact that many off-world colonies suffer from plagues that always require serums stored on far-distant planets. We won't even ask why the colonies in peril never send a subspace message asking for the replicator data necessary for the needed serum!

credibility that Captains as brilliant and astute as Janeway and Picard wouldn't impose stricter security measures on their vessels. But the demands of television force us to believe that ship security is one subject not taught at Starfleet Academy.

Though Federation starships are equipped with the most powerful computers ever constructed, this technology isn't being used to strike an appropriate balance between ship safety and individual privacy and freedom. It's difficult to believe that in the twenty-third and twenty-fourth centuries, these problems wouldn't have long ago been solved. Each of the described predicaments could be neutralized using technology displayed in *Star Trek*—and with computer software in development today.

Too often, onboard security personnel are put at risk, even killed hunting alien intruders or guarding dangerous prisoners. These tasks would be handled better and more safely by the ship's computer. Keeping the starship secure shouldn't be difficult for a computer network already programmed to monitor life-support systems, maintain engine stability, and operate the communications array.

On the original *Enterprise*, carrying over four hundred people, intruders often blend in with the crew or hide in remote sections of the ship. The ship is even invaded by Federation officers from the future ("Trials and Tribblations," *DS9*), who interact with the crew and captain without detection.

Once, Captain Kirk is actually framed for murder by a crewmember who fakes his own death then keeps out of sight in the ship's engineering decks ("Court Martial," *TOS*). When Kirk finally realizes what's happened, he uses the ship's computer to track down the criminal. It's obvious from the astonished reactions of the tribunal that such an activity has never been done before. Which makes sense by television logic, because otherwise there would be no plot. With minor modifications, the same programs could be adapted to keep the starship free of any unwanted guests.

The *Enterprise* computer system is capable of monitoring and recording all conversations taking place on the ship and playing them back for authorized personnel ("Turnabout Intruder," *TOS*). Using consoles and communication posts scattered throughout the ship, the computer can even detect the heartbeats of every person on board ("Court Martial," *TOS*). Furthermore, it can be programmed to block out specific heartbeats. Kirk proves there's an unauthorized person on the *Enterprise* by progressively blocking out the heartbeats of everyone known to be on board. Finally, when there should be silence, one heartbeat remains.

As we've noted, all starship crewmembers and visitors wear communicator badges. The computer system can use this badge to determine the location of anyone anywhere on the ship. These ID badges could easily be linked into the ship's transportation system, making it impossible to travel from one sector of the vessel to another without proper identification.

A simple combination of these few programs would result in a very basic but quite dependable security system. Here's how it would operate.

The ship's computer would constantly oversee all crewmembers' locations by their badges, matching their locations with a map of the ship. At the same time, the computer would continually monitor heartbeats throughout the vessel. More heartbeats than communicators would indicate intruders on the *Enterprise*. Any local excess of either heartbeats or communicators would be noted by the computer, and in the event of an intrusion, these areas of mismatch would be sealed off by force fields. As an additional backup, the computer system could immediately check all conversations taking place in that area, identifying all voices logged into the communications network, and sorting out any that aren't on file.

This program would work for all beings having hearts. Given the sophistication of the *Enterprise* computer system, it could certainly be modified to detect other, equally distinctive sounds that would betray any alien presence on the ship. This extremely simple system makes only limited use of the ship's internal sensors, which could easily identify every crewmember and guest by his or her unique chemical signature (as a dog does) or by the "bioelectric field." The Federation probably would refrain from such intrusive monitoring out of respect for privacy.

Anyone not wearing a communicator badge would immediately be identified by the computer system as an intruder. Without an ID, that being could not travel from deck to deck or section to section. Forcefields could be employed by the computer to immediately imprison the intruder ("Brothers," *TNG*). It could even be arranged that none of the ship's amenities—doors, lights, replicators, and other functions—would work for a person without a badge. Badges would also be coded by rank to prevent unauthorized personnel from entering secure areas. As a visitor, Ralph Offenhouse could never have simply walked onto the bridge during a tense standoff with the Romulans. ("The Neutral Zone," *TNG*) Something like this system is used on the starships of the twenty-fourth century though it appears to function erratically.

Any such system, however, would compromise personal privacy. Secret rendezvous for whatever purpose would be impossible. Equally chilling would be the knowledge that the ship's computer is monitoring all communication and possibly recording the most intimate and private conversations. Despite undoubtedly strict limits on the use of such information, the fact remains that any person on board can be spied on to an almost unlimited extent, all of the time. Even with the best intentions, life must be a strain. For example, a captain who gave the crew even the slightest reason to doubt his integrity might find it impossible to lead.

Personal privacy could be protected by a series of safeguards on the computer system. For example, suppose the ship's computer has a malfunction and is acting strangely (a fairly common *Trek* plot line). Worf and Chief O'Brien must shut it down and fix it. But Chief O'Brien knows that, quite often, he has trouble with the artificially intelligent ship's computer, which seems to have a mind of its own. He and Worf require absolute privacy. The computer must not know what they're plotting. Worf and O'Brien need only deactivate the computer's ability to record their conversations. Their voice prints and DNA patterns, to name only two examples, should presumably suffice to identify them to the computer and grant them the required privacy. Still, a computer capable of generating a Professor Moriarity might decide to disobey them, if it was malfunctioning.

Regardless, privacy issues would still exist, as they already do in holosuites and holodecks. Though the holosuites are commonly used to for exercise and relaxation, they do represent a possible privacy concern. Perhaps Quark programmed a holosuite for a romantic interlude with an imaginary version of Dax. To protect his privacy, Quark would keep the program on a "disk" or even delete it after every use. Still, disks can be stolen, disks can be copied, and any competent computer engineer could program the holosuite computer to save secret files of all deleted programs.

Another danger of holosuites is the distinct possibility that users could become so strongly attached to holocreated characters to threaten their mental health. Though rarely discussed, holosuites could cause major emotional or psychological problems for distraught or lonely individuals (Reg Barclay in "Hollow Pursuits," *TNG*; Harry Kim in "Alter Ego," *VGR*).

Still, if anything, the ship's computer as programmed in the twenty-fourth century is too protective of individual privacy. Though the *Enterprise* computer can pinpoint the location of any individual on the ship, it doesn't unless specifically asked. (The same appears true of all Starfleet ship computers and the system on *Deep Space Nine.*) When Captain Picard is kidnapped from his quarters by Q, the computer doesn't alert the crew that he is missing ("Q Who?" *TNG*). This lack of concern seems to be carrying personal privacy to an extreme.

On the other hand, twenty-fourth century values are sure to be very different from ours. The people of the real twenty-fourth century may well have a fetish for privacy that we would view as irrational. Yet exactly what they consider private might seem very strange to us.

Communicator badges and sound recognition software aren't the only solutions to ship's security. A number of other identification systems are in development today that would work just as easily. Biometrics is the name given to the field of using a computer to verify an individual's identity based on unique biological traits. While biometric methods are based on human characteristics, it isn't a far leap to imagine that three centuries in the future, biometrics will have advanced to identify aliens as well as Terrans.

Security concerns continue to grow as crime and fraud grow increasingly sophisticated as we approach the twenty-first century. The United States government has established a focal point for biometric research called the Biometric Consortium. Over a hundred different high-tech companies are registered with the Consortium, each vying to develop a fool-proof method of determining a person's identity. Spain uses biometrics to identify people qualified for unemployment and medical benefits. In the United States, the immigration system and various hospitals use biometrics. Russia plans to use biometrics in its banking systems, and France and Germany plan to use biometrics on credit cards. Several countries are even using DNA as a biometric identification technique. Many countries plan to use these systems for everything from social security and banking systems to election and polling control. The problems of security in the future that we've discussed in this chapter are already a major concern today.

The most common form of biometrics, and the one in use in secure installations throughout the world today is fingerprint recognition. The chance of two people having the same fingerprint is less than one in a billion. Biometric finger scanners merely require a person to place a finger onto a computer screen for a second. Surprisingly, the fingerprint is not analyzed by the whorls of the print (as seen in numerous police and FBI shows over the decades) but by a computerized picture of the finger comprised of tens of thousands of small dots mapping the skin. In a fairly short interval, this pattern can be compared to millions of fingerprints on file and ensure positive identification of the individual.

Of course, such a system isn't perfect. As suggested by more than one gruesome crime drama, fingerprint analysis doesn't work if the finger being analyzed isn't attached to the proper hand. Nor is there a national, much less world-wide fingerprint data bank available to determine wanted criminals. But because of its speed and low cost, biometric fingerprint identification has become commonplace in many banks and financial institutions.

A somewhat more sophisticated system used at institutions that require more rigid security (such as nuclear power plants, government laboratories, high-tech military installations) is the Biometric Handshape Recognition scanner. The name of the device makes clear its function. Individuals working at the installation put their hand inside a scanner and multiple cameras working in conjunction with an advanced computer program map a three-dimensional image of the hand. According to the developers of this technology, the exact shapes of hands differ and confirmation of an individual's identity is fool-proof. Of course, the system only works when comparing the hand-print to those on file, and is relatively time consuming.

A third method of biometric identification is popular in James Bond films, European banks, and a few top-secret installations. It is iris prints, where an infra-red light scans a person's iris and matches the scan against a print on file. According to the Biometric Consortium, iris scans are more accurate than DNA tests. Unfortunately, most people object to having their eyes scanned by infra-red beams and this method of identification is costly and unpopular.

Perhaps the most promising system of biometric identification is facial recognition technology. NVisage from Neurodynamics uses a combination of cameras and computers to form a three-dimensional scan of a person's face that can be made in full light or complete darkness. This identification method is popular because of all the biometric techniques, it is the least intrusive and can be done without the person being aware of the action. In a future where computers and scanners will be built into the walls of a starship, facial recognition would be a natural method of maintaining security.

Another promising technique presently under development is bodynets—identification of the unique electric auras that surround people. Still in the basic developmental stages are ID chips planted in a person's hand that would automatically open doors and trigger proper security codes in research centers. Similar research is being done involving nanochips that would be injected into people's fingertips.

Whatever evolves, security on Federation starships will be much more advanced than anything we can imagine at the moment. But no security system will ever be absolutely flawless. Consider that the transporter can instantly do a full-body scan and duplicate a person's unique DNA pattern. Transporter malfunctions created two Captain Kirks ("The Enemy Within," *TOS*), and two Commander Rikers ("Second Chances," *TNG*). Unless human nature changes over the next three centuries, most likely every innovation in security will be matched by a new technique to thwart it. Still, whether the ship's crew numbers in the hundreds (as on the original *Enterprise*), or over a thousand (the *Enterprise-D* of the twenty-fourth century), there's no reason that any of them should be at risk from intruders. Unfortunately, guaranteeing the safety of the starship's computer core isn't so easy.

Having Jem'Hadar warriors beam onto the bridge of the *Defiant* with drawn phasers might make for good TV, but it is not the most likely method of attacking the ship. An assault on the starship's computer mainframe is much more promising. And a lot less risky.

The Romulans and the Borg have been tough, deadly *Star Trek* foes. But the Bynaars captured the *Enterprise* without firing a shot. ("10010011," *TNG*)

In the trusting *Star Trek* world of the twenty-third and twenty-fourth centuries, no one seems to worry about viruses or malignant programs until it's too late. Messages and files are routinely downloaded to starship and space station computer cores. Precautions against viruses may be in place, but if they are, they're not very effective as demonstrated by numerous incidents of code alteration that happen to the starship's main computer and the holodeck computer system. And viruses are only one of the electronic dangers facing Federation computers.

Many scientists believe that the wars of the future will be fought primarily between computer systems, not on battlefields. They feel that destroying the enemy's computer network would cause greater destruction than any bomb or biological weapon. The more advanced a society, the more vulnerable it'll be to computer warfare. Thus, the technologically dependent Federation would be a prime target for computer terrorists.

In the twenty-fourth century, sabotaging an electrical grid ("Homefront," *DS9*) or tampering with a security program ("Civil Defense," *DS9*) would be a cost effective and extremely deadly method of fighting. One person hacking into a computer network could affect billions. Hackers would be a constant danger on planets or installations where they would be able to focus their attack on large systems, tapping in unnoticed and downloading important information or tampering with system security ("Babel," *DS9*). Still, hacking into a starship or space-station computer wouldn't be easy, especially since the network is a closed system where any intrusions are quickly noted ("Babel" *DS9*, "Meridian," *DS9*, "The Quest," *TNG*).

Other methods of attacking *Star Trek* computer systems would be more insidious and harder to detect. While a fleet of Klingon starships might not be able to conquer *Deep Space Nine*, a few lines of computer code could. The main weapons used in such attacks would include worms, Trojan horses, and the most infamous of all destructive programs, the computer virus. Hidden in an innocent-seeming transmission to a starship, they could cause catastrophic damage.

A computer worm is a program that uses flaws and holes in a network's operating system to gain access to machines and duplicate itself again and again. Worms are self sufficient; they don't need to attach themselves to another computer program to exist. They gobble up computer space and thus absorb system's resources. In 1988, a computer worm spread through thousands of computer systems hooked to the Internet in just a few days. Imagine what it could do to the Federation's network, linking hundreds of planets and thousands of starships. Furthermore, worms can be programmed to explode into life months after they infect systems.

A Trojan-horse program appears to perform a specific and useful function, but it also has a hidden, usually destructive, agenda.

It's different from a computer virus in that it doesn't reproduce and infect other computers. The "Babel" program that caused the replicators on *Deep Space Nine* to produce a deadly virus ("Babel," *DS9*) is a perfect example of a Trojan-horse program.

Trojan-horse programs are extremely dangerous because they can be hidden in an operating system for long periods of time, unnoticed by anyone, until a specific chain of events sets them into operation. The deadly Cardassian security program that nearly destroys *Deep Space Nine* acts much like a Trojan-horse program. It is activated by events that no longer have any meaning on the station, but nearly succeeds in destroying all life on *Deep Space Nine* before it is deactivated ("Civil Defense," *DS9*).

The ultimate Trojan-horse program in the *Star Trek* universe has to be the code found in an 87-million-year-old artifact located in the nucleus of a comet in the D'Arsay system. The incredibly ancient program is downloaded to the *Enterprise-D* computer and takes over the ship's systems. The code uses the computer to recreate episodes of D'Arsay mythology, endangering the lives of everyone aboard the starship ("Masks," *TNG*).

Worms and Trojan-horse programs can be dangerous, oftentimes deadly. Neither, however, is as harmful as a computer virus.

The simplest definition of a computer virus is a program that changes other programs so as to include a working copy of itself inside them. Most computer viruses have a secondary, often malevolent, purpose. Most are coded to spread to as many machines as possible. In many ways, computer viruses are extremely similar to their biological cousins.

Just as a biological virus needs a cell to reproduce, a computer virus needs another program for the same reason. Infected cells, like infected programs, can continue to function for a long time without showing any sign of the virus. Once a biological cell's been infected, it makes new copies of the virus to infect other cells. A program infected by a computer virus creates new copies of the virus to infect other programs. Most important, after a certain incubation period, a virus attacks the living system containing the infected cell. Just as a computer virus attacks the system containing the corrupted program. More than one researcher has pointed out that computer viruses could almost be classified as artificial life.

Over the past decades, hundreds of new viruses have been detected and neutralized. Still, rogue programmers continue to manufacture malignant code that they release onto the Internet. And, with the increased globalization of computer technology, their aims have become increasingly dangerous.

According to *Time* magazine, during the Gulf War, a band of Dutch hackers asked Iraq for one million dollars to disrupt the U.S. military's deployment in the Middle East. No details of their plans were revealed. Fortunately for the United States, the Iraqis turned them down. Considering that the U.S. military uses the Internet for communications, the hackers could have caused serious problems for Operation Desert Storm.[1]

The Department of Defense considers cyberwar one of the greatest threats of the twenty-first century. It's difficult to believe the threat will have disappeared by the twenty-fourth century. The computer systems of Federation starships and space stations seem extremely vulnerable to the most basic incursions and disruptions. The faith crewmembers and station personnel place in such systems appears to be terribly naïve. Too often, major programs such as those involving the replicator, the transporter, and the holodeck crash, causing major disasters.

A more serious problem was noted in Chapter 2. The three computer cores of the *Enterprise* are linked by faster-than-light (FTL) transmitters so that they're always 100 percent redundant. What one computer knows, all three know. That's fine if, in the midst of a space battle, the main computer core is hit by phaser fire. The engineering computer core would immediately take control of the ship's defenses and weapons. Even a few nanoseconds can matter in a fight conducted between ships moving at impulse speeds. Still, that redundancy can be awfully dangerous if the enemy's using a virus instead of a photon torpedo.

If the three computer cores are working at FTL speeds and are 100 percent redundant, a virus imported to one core will immediately infect all three. Filters and anti-virus programs offer some degree of protection, but if they can't protect the ship's main computer, as they often can't, how can they protect the backup systems that are set for instantaneous data duplication? Total redundancy would lead to total disaster. Computer viruses are mostly ignored on *Star Trek*. They shouldn't be.

Which brings us to our final topic involving computer security in the twenty-fourth century, the subject that's the center of any discussion of involving military or government security today—encryption. It's important now, and there's no indication that three hundred years from now it still won't be important.

Basically, encryption is writing a message in code so it can't be read by anyone other than its intended recipient. Secret codes have been popular in fiction ever since Poe's "The Gold Bug" and Conan Doyle's "The Musgrave Ritual." Breaking the Nazi code in World War II was an important factor in defeating the Third Reich. While the government and military are prime users of encryption, it's also used by businesses and industries throughout the world to protect financial information as well as sensitive data. Obviously, the best encryption system is one that can't be broken by outsiders. Not surprisingly, modern encryption techniques involve computers.

In simple terms, encryption disguises a message so it can only be understood by someone authorized to read it. The original message, called *plaintext*, looks like ordinary text. The encryption process typically uses one or more *keys*, which are mathematical algorithms that change the plaintext into *ciphertext*—what looks like garbled numbers, letters, and symbols. After decryption by the authorized reader of the message, the ciphertext returns to its original form, plaintext.

Encryption, like other methods of computer security, can also open systems to abuse. If you think that you're transmitting a message that's totally encrypted, you might send extremely sensitive data across a network. Suppose someone intercepts your encrypted message and hacks the key you used to turn it into ciphertext. Your sensitive data is at the mercy of the wrong people. Think about transactions that typically occur today. Lots of people do online banking. Many people purchase items on the Internet. Many people trade stocks online. A very small number of these transactions are encrypted as they course the phone lines and travel from computer server to computer server along the global net.

With all the talk about encryption, it's worthwhile to point out that very few people use it. You may have PGP keys*, but nobody you know wants to learn PGP and obtain their own keys. One guy doesn't have time to study the manual, which admittedly, takes a good amount of effort. Another is afraid that his wife will accuse him of sending and receiving adulterous emails if she finds encrypted letters on his computer! There are probably dozens of legitimate reasons why people don't bother with encryption.

Personally, we favor strong encryption to protect privacy as much as we can. But this points to the general debate that's been raging for years about encryption. Some people, like us, think it's critical to our future security. Other people, like governments, think that encryption will allow bad guys to transmit secret messages about bank heists, murders, and government revolutions.[2]

---

* Pretty Good Privacy, discussed later in this chapter.

At the present time, almost any encryption method can be hacked by brute force. This means that a programmer tries all possible key values until he finds the correct one.

If a key is eight bits long, there are 2^8 or 256 possible keys. Using a programming technique that halves the possibilities and searches only the appropriate branches of a tree for a match, we guess that someone could crack the key after approximately 128 attempts.

But if an 8-bit key has 2^8 possible keys, then a 64-bit key has 2^{64} possible keys and a 128-bit key has 2^{128} possible keys. Bruce Schneier, the king of cryptography, says that it would take a supercomputer 585,000 years to find a correct key among 2^{64} possibilities and 10^{25} years to find it among 2^{128} possibilities. [3] He also points out that the universe is 10^{10} years old. On the flip side, Mr. Schneier says that most large companies and criminal organizations have the resources to crack a 56-bit key, and that most military budgets suffice to crack a 64-bit key. He predicts that within thirty years, it'll be possible to break 80-bit keys.

Within a hundred years, our current technology will be dust. Hardware will change dramatically into DNA, optical, holographic, and/or quantum forms. And software will change to fit its new hosts. Methods of cryptography will change along with the hardware and software. Who knows how long it'll take a DNA computer, for example, to crack a 128-bit key coded in flesh rather than metal registers? It might be a quick job using a quantum-level computer.

In the time of *Star Trek*, nanotech implants in our bodies will dictate entirely new methods of encryption. Possibly a chemical method based on our neurotransmissions. Or an algorithm based on our blood chemistry. Or on our genetic makeup.

However, the basic cracking technique will remain the same: infiltrate and break the code. Imagine having a computer function infiltrate your body and attack your implanted body network identity chip. No doubt you'll have a mechanism to fight the disease of infiltration, much as our blood fights infections today. Tiny nanotech-manufactured devices will scour your bloodstream, find all attacking cracker code, and eat it.

In summary, today's encryption methods are not terribly relevant to the world of *Star Trek*. The use of "fractal encryption algorithms" by Data is absurd. Just more technobabble to make the show sound futuristic and serious.

For the curious, here's a brief summary of the state of current encryption technology. For details, we suggest that you study not only *Applied Cryptography* by Bruce Schneier, but also recent articles in magazines such as *Dr. Dobb's*.

Symmetric encryption means that both the sender and receiver of information use the same secret key. The Data Encryption Standard (DES) is the most famous example of symmetric encryption. DES uses a 56-bit key applied to 64-bit blocks of data. DES is still in widespread use in the banking community. In July of 1998, the Electronic Frontier Foundation at http://www.eff.org reported that it had created a $220,000 computer that could break a DES key in four and a half days. For people who believe in Moore's Law, this means that the DES-cracking machine will cost $110,000 in five years, and it might crack the key in two days. Further, in the landmark *The Electronic Privacy Papers*, coauthored by Mr. Schneier and David Banisar, it's noted that "Within a few years, experts anticipate that DES will no longer be secure from even low-level attacks." [4]

Another symmetric technique is triple DES, which inputs three 56-bit keys to an array of three DES chips. Triple-DES is supposedly too slow for various applications. Then there's IDEA, which uses a 128-bit key on 64-bit blocks of data.

In January of 1997, hoping to replace DES, the National Institute of Standards and Technology (NIST) asked for a new Advanced Encryption Standard (AES). In June of 1998, fifteen encryption algorithms were submitted for review. At the time of the millenium—scheduled for January of 2000—the final AES will be chosen to replace DES. [5]

One of the really cool things about the AES contest is that three of the submissions have already been cracked.

It's amusing to note the names of the encryption techniques, as reported by Mr. Schneier (his comments are in quotes): [6]

> *CAST–256.* Slower than other AES submissions.
>
> *LOCKI–97.* Already cracked.
>
> *Frog.* Already cracked.
>
> *Mars.* "IBM gave the world DES, and Mars is its submission to AES . . . the pedigree and impressive design document make this a strong candidate despite its 'kitchen sink' appearance."
>
> *Magenta.* Already cracked.
>
> *RC6.* From Ron Rivest at RSA Data Security, Inc.
>
> *Decorrelated Fast Cipher (DFC).*
>
> *Serpent.*
>
> *E2.*
>
> *Rijndael.*
>
> *DEAL.* A variety of triple-DES.
>
> *Hasty Pudding Cipher (HPC).* "Take everything you can think of, throw it in a cipher, shake well, then add some attitude. 'Bizarre' is all I can say."
>
> *Crypton.*
>
> *Twofish.*
>
> *SAFER+.*

We mention RC6, so we should also mention its predecessors. All come from RSA, which is not only the name of Ron Rivest's company but also the name of yet another encryption technique. RC, in the wonderful world of computer acronyms, stands for Ron's Code. It also stands for Rivest Cipher. RC1, missing from the list, was a design that flopped. RC3, also missing, was cracked before it was released. RC2 uses a variable-length key on a 64-bit block of data. RC4 is the same as RC2, except the former is a stream cipher (operates on the plaintext one bit or one byte at a time) rather than a block cipher (operates on the plaintext in blocks of data). RC5 permits you to change the block size, key length, and the number of iterations used for encryption. The RC algorithms are all symmetric encryption techniques.

RSA, on the other hand, is an asymmetric technique, also known as a public key approach. This means that the encryption key differs from the decryption key—often called the private key. RSA multiplies two huge prime numbers to obtain its decryption key. Factoring the key using today's computers could require several billion years.

PGP combines IDEA for encryption, RSA for key management and digital signatures, and MD5 for hashing functions.

So what is MD5? There are more encryption techniques than fleas on a dog. Before MD5, we had MD2 and MD4. All were created by Ron Rivest of RSA, Ron Rivest's company. And even if we told you about MD5 and hashing, you still wouldn't know about Blowfish and Twofish. Or Panama.

In the not-so-distant future, it's hypothetically possible that a digitally encrypted transmission could be further encrypted with the fingerprint of the receiver. Thus, only the specific person being sent the message would be able to read it. But if this technique becomes common, hackers will quickly develop methods to duplicate fingerprints—

Hey, haven't criminals done that already?

Only when biometrics reach the level of nanotech will we see real biometric encryption—in three or four hundred years.

In *Star Trek*, messages between starships and their bases, and between crewmembers and their ships, are encrypted before transmission. The coding technique is never mentioned. The encryption algorithm is no doubt far more advanced than today's methods. Still, the *Trek* encryption codes are clearly imperfect. The self-destruct code on two versions of the *Enterprise* rely on voice recognition, surely not a very secure encryption technique (as demonstrated by Data in several instances). The Borg, as evidenced by Seven-of-Nine, have little trouble breaking *Voyager's* encryption codes ("Scorpion" and all episodes that follow, *VGR*). While the Borg are a unique race, there's no reason to believe that their skill at encryption is unmatched. Garak, on *Deep Space Nine*, often breaks Cardassian encrypted messages for the Federation. Arturis, a member of Species 116 ("Hope and Fear," *VGR*) is shown as adept or even more talented at breaking codes (including those of the Federation) than the Borg.

How best to manage these security problems? Present-day hackers have proven again and again that no program, however sophisticated, is invulnerable to attack, that no code is unbreakable. It's difficult to believe that this situation will change over the next few centuries. We suspect three hundred years from now the methods might change somewhat, but that the problems of security will remain the same.

Navigation
and Battle

When Captain Picard, on the bridge of the *Enterprise*, receives an emergency message from the Federation science station on Ventax II (in "Devil's Due," *TNG*), he immediately instructs Wesley Crusher to lay in a course for that planet at maximum warp. Wesley pushes a few buttons, and Picard tells him to "engage." Off they go.

What exactly is Wesley doing? The ship's computer handles all of the calculations involved in plotting the course, laying in the coordinates, and setting the starship into motion. At best, Wesley just punches in the name of their destination, like a counter attendant at Burger King, and the computer does the rest. There's no actual reason for the captain to do anything more than speak, other than that it may satisfy Starfleet regulations. The helmsman and pilot on Federation starships serve no purpose aside from tradition.

Any meaningful discussion of space navigation requires acknowledging two facts:

create

Navigation and Battle

1. Light travels at approximately 300,000 kilometers/second (around 186,000 miles/second).
2. Space is BIG. For example, the nearest star to Earth, Alpha Centauri, is 4.3 light years away, with a light year being the distance light travels in a year ($9.46 * 10^{12}$ kilometers). The sun, 149.6 million kilometers from Earth, is a little more than 8 light minutes away.

Size and speed are the reasons the ship's computer handles interstellar navigation. Because space is so vast and light travels so fast, we need pinpoint accuracy traveling through the void. Close isn't good enough when we're talking about warp drive shooting our ship at many times faster than 300,000 kilometers per second. The smallest mistake could plunge a starship into a nearby sun— or far more likely, send it hurtling billions of miles beyond our destination. Navigation in outer space requires precision impossible to achieve other than with computer-generated exactness.

Yet ship captains have managed to steer their vessels across Earth's oceans from one port to another with reasonable accuracy for hundreds of years—without the benefit of computers. Ocean of water, ocean of stars, what's the difference?

Obviously, the size of the ocean.

Outer space is so incredibly vast, so immense, it's difficult to express distance in a manner that makes sense.

The Atlantic Ocean is approximately 4,025 kilometers wide. Let's say we are flying in a straight path across the Earth's surface (a curved line known as a geodesic, since our world is a globe) from point A in London to point B in New York City. If for every kilometer we travel, we deviate off our path by one millimeter (1/1,000,000 of a kilometer), we'd end up in New York City approximately 4 meters from our destination. That's quite acceptable for such a trip.

Now, let's travel from point A in London to point C on an imagined planet in the Alpha Centauri star system, 4.3 light years away. Given that a light year is 9.46×10^{12} kilometers, 4.3 light years is approximately 40×10^{12} kilometers. If we deviate off course by that same millimeter for every kilometer we travel, we'd arrive approximately 40 million kilometers off target.* That's about the distance from Earth to Venus. Or about fifty round trips between the Earth and the Moon.

In interstellar terms, that's not terrible. At normal impulse speed, it would take the *Enterprise* a little less than ten minutes to reach point C. Not bad. But we suspect Captain Picard would find the delay unacceptable. Especially when that serum needs to be delivered.

Let's consider a somewhat more typical trip: a routine mission to a Federation outpost that's four weeks from Earth traveling at Warp 6—approximately 300 times the speed of light. Assuming the same error as before, 1 millimeter off for every kilometer traveled, the *Enterprise* would drop out of warp approximately a billion kilometers from the outpost. Almost the distance from Saturn to the sun: four hours' travel at maximum impulse. Captain Picard surely would not be pleased.

Simply put, the tiniest navigation errors become magnified by the vast distances involved in traveling through the galaxy. Speed and distance are so great that normal degrees of measurement become meaningless.

Yet only rarely do we see helm control explicitly turned over to the computer. Consider the *Deep Space Nine* episode "A Time to Stand." Sisko and his crew guide a stolen Jem'Hadar starship to a

---

* If for each kilometer, we are one millimeter off, then we're off approximately 4×10^{10} meters, or 4×10^7 kilometers—in very approximate terms, 40 million kilometers.

Dominion storage facility. The plan is to blow up the base, disrupting Dominion war activities. Sisko and friends manage to plant a bomb on the base. That's when Chief O'Brien warns that the explosion will destroy everything within a radius of 800 kilometers. Unfortunately, as the ship prepares to go to warp speed, the base raises its security shield, trapping them close to the asteroid surface.

The only way for them to escape, the Captain realizes, is to be traveling directly at the security barrier when the bomb blows up the base and takes out the shield's power generator. Using the computer, Dax calculates they must accelerate to impulse speed exactly 1.3 seconds before the blast. Sisko turns piloting controls of the ship over to the main computer to ensure perfect timing. It's a rare admission by the Captain that sometimes human reflexes aren't accurate enough for interstellar navigation.

Too bad the details as stated by the crew don't make any sense. The barrier around the base obviously is less than 800 kilometers from the asteroid, otherwise Sisko wouldn't be worried about the blast. But impulse speed is 75,000 kilometers per second. Having the computer bring the ship to full impulse 1.3 seconds before the blast would instantly flatten the ship against the forcefield. Better to accelerate at 0.001 seconds before the blast. That's not a problem for a computer that calculates in nanoseconds. But it's quite impossible for human senses and reflexes.

The history of *Star Trek* does offer a possible reason for this massive distrust of computerized space war. An early attempt to test a supercomputer named M-5 as commander of the *Enterprise* in a battle situation resulted in disaster ("The Ultimate Computer," *TOS*). A hundred years later, when Data created the android, Lal, Starfleet command viewed his work with suspicion, citing the M-5 disaster. They wanted the work stopped.

It's difficult to believe that the *Star Trek* writers could have been so traumatized by the M-5 incident that they halted an entire field of scientific endeavor. Still, genetic engineering seems to have been outlawed for three hundred years by the Federation ("Doctor Bashir, I Presume," *DS9*) because of the eugenics experiments of the late twentieth century that resulted in the creation of Khan Noonien Singh. People (like Dr. Bashir's father) are sent to prison for violating these laws, even if done without malice. The universe of *Star Trek* does have its illogical aspects.

With that thought firmly in mind, let's consider the much more complex problem of a full-scale war in outer space. This has always been one of the mainstays of science fiction. Great battles between opposing star systems have filled the pages of science-fiction magazines for as long as there have been science-fiction magazines. Scholarly articles were even written on the subject, such as "Space War," published in 1939, in which the noted rocket scientist and science writer Willy Ley discussed possible weapons for spaceships. He concluded that ordinary cannons using explosive shells would be quite effective because, to save weight, ships wouldn't be heavily armored. Though these early studies were detailed and intelligently presented, none of the writers could guess the amazing advances that would occur in the physical sciences in the next half century. Nor did any science-fiction writer predict the astonishing revolution that would take place in cybernetics.

Some of the best episodes of both *Deep Space Nine* and *Voyager* have dealt with battles in the interstellar void. As when *Voyager* encountered the Borg battling Species 8472 in "Scorpion." Or even more interesting, the huge space battle with the Dominion shown in *Deep Space Nine* adventures "Favor the Bold" and "Sacrifice of Angels."

In the latter episode, Commander Sisko leads a fleet of six hundred Federation starships on a desperate last minute mission to free *Deep Space Nine* from the forces of the Dominion. However, an armada of more than twelve hundred enemy ships blocks Sisko's path. The commander states that the only way to save *Deep Space Nine*, and thus the Alpha Quadrant, is to punch a hole through the Dominion fleet so that the Federation starships can get to the station. The collision of the two fleets and the ensuing conflict make for exciting television. But none of it makes much sense.

Consider the Dominion blockade that Sisko must somehow force his way past. This conflict isn't a naval battle or even a dogfight between jet planes. It's war in space.

According to *Star Trek* technical lore, phasers have a range of 300,000 kilometers, and their power fades significantly over long distances. As coherent energy beams, they obey the inverse square law, so the farther the target, the less effect the beam will have. Suppose the twelve hundred Dominion ships were deployed in a square, thirty-five ships to a side. A formation tight enough to blast any vessel trying to get through would make the square approximately 10 million kilometers on a side. That's a pretty big blockade. But when starships moving at impulse speed travel at 75,000 kilometers per second, it's nowhere near big enough. Why fight when you can go around? A Federation ship could fly the entire length of this blockade in 133 seconds. Not much of a detour. It's as if the German High Command had tried to stop the invasion of Normandy by building a ten-foot-high wall the length of a tennis court on Omaha Beach.

Nor does Sisko's fleet have to travel merely at impulse speed. Why not just accelerate to Warp 2 (10 times the speed of light), zip around the blockade in 3.3 seconds, and head off to *Deep Space Nine*? Even easier, why not just fly at Warp 2 or better between the enemy ships? Phaser beams propagate at the speed of light. A ship traveling faster than light would be gone before the enemy even knew it was there, and the phaser beam would never catch up.*

---

* This raises the interesting question of why a ship capable of warp speed would need a cloaking device. If the signals detected by sensors travel at the

Engaging fleet against fleet in outer space makes little sense. It's reminiscent of those stylized Revolutionary War battles in which opposing armies knelt in straight lines to fire at each other across a green meadow. But sending a fleet in a group to save the station made no sense anyway. A more intelligent strategy would have six hundred ships approaching the station from six hundred directions. Traveling at different warp speeds, coming in on many different paths, using cloaked ships, the dynamics of battle would tax the most elaborate defense strategy. The entire Dominion fleet would have a hard time coping with such an attack. And no human mind could choreograph it—but a computer could.

Battles between opposing fleets make no sense unless one of the fleets is guarding a location, such as a planet or space station. Even then, the human element in such a battle would be insignificant. Computers will fight the wars in space, not men. Human reflexes are too slow. In space war, there's no time to issue commands like "Raise shields" or "Fire on my mark." If you report that "they're powering weapons," the news is already too late by the time the words are out of your mouth. Talking doesn't work when events are moving at nanosecond speed.

Suppose we're on a routine exploration mission. The ship has just emerged from warp drive at the edge of an unknown solar system. Life signs are detected by the long-range sensors on the fourth planet of the solar system and you, as captain, order the ship to approach the world at full impulse power (1/4 the speed of light, 75,000 km/sec). Being cautious, you put the ship on yellow alert. Shields are immediately raised and phasers armed.

As the ship approaches the green and blue world, an enemy ship swings out from behind its moon, approximately 300,000

speed of light, you'd never detect a ship approaching at warp speed until it was well past. FTL speed serves as its own cloak. Most ships wisely use cloaking devices when traveling at impulse speed, well below light speed.

kilometers away, the farthest range for phaser attack. It instantly attacks. The next few ticks of the clock are filled with action.

Phasers operate at the speed of light. From 300,000 kilometers away, it takes the fire from the enemy ship one second to strike our shields. The shields flare but hold. Reacting in milliseconds to the energy burst, our ship's computer takes control of the helm and accelerates the ship in evasive maneuvers. At the same time, the computer's artificial-intelligence battle program goes into action.

The enemy vessel is moving at impulse speed, 1/4 the speed of light. Though the signals detected by the sensors travel at light speed, there's no way to track the attackers. If the ship is 150,000 kilometers away, it would take the sensors a half-second to detect its position, then another half-second for the phaser fire to reach its target—a total of one second. During that second, the enemy will have traveled another 75,000 kilometers, probably not in a straight line. These are ships that accelerate to ten times the speed of light in the time it takes to fade to a commercial; they can literally turn on a dime. (To prevent the crew from being squashed to jelly by the accelerations involved in such maneuvers, they have something called "inertial dampers.") In theory, the enemy could be anywhere within a sphere of radius 75,000 kilometers—a volume of 400 trillion cubic kilometers, or a space big enough to hold 2,000 Earth-size planets. In this situation the idea of having weapons "locked on target," as they so often are in *Star Trek* space battles, is meaningless. The ships are moving too fast, over too huge a volume of space, for sensors to do any good.

One reason computers must handle the battle is that people can't react in milliseconds. In space war, there's no time to hesitate, no time to blink, no time to sweat. But there's another reason that has nothing to do with speed.

Controlled by computer, our ship's phaser bank spreads an array of beams 150,000 kilometers ahead of the enemy's last known position. The battle has become a guessing game. With the helm completely under the computer's control, the ship continually veers from its original course, trying to maneuver the enemy into a position where its options are reduced. In the meantime, the attackers aren't waiting for us to act. Less than a second after the first exchange of phaser fire, they shoot again but miss. Our computer, programmed with thousands of combat simulations, has analyzed and compared the situation to similar encounters. An artifical-intelligence program has extrapolated the course the enemy expected us to take and avoids it. It's a battle between two computers. Humans don't matter. If anything, they're a danger.

People are too predictable. They tend to react in certain ways to danger. That's why boxers study films of their opponent's fights. Habits developed over years are difficult to break. A computer programmed to change course randomly won't always resort to "Attack Pattern Omega" when the ship is fired on. Reacting predictably to an attack, showing any kind of pattern or tendency, would be instantly detected by a computer programmed to detect just such behavior and use it to direct phaser fire. The safest path is a random one, and only computers can act (almost) randomly.

Our phasers fire again, again in a wide-spread array, hoping to catch the adversary as it shifts position. Another hit. The enemy's computer isn't programmed as well as our computer. It follows a fairly unsophisticated battle plan. Their shields flare then go dead. A moment later, their ship explodes. In space battles, there is no chance to surrender.

The entire fight lasts less than five seconds. No chance to yell "Shields up!" In space, once a battle begins, there is no time for talking. Sorry, but human reflexes can't react to beams traveling at the speed of light. No one can steer a spaceship moving at 75,000 kilometers per second and successfully avoid phaser fire traveling at light speed. No human can analyze thousands of attack possibilities and choose the best one in less than a millisecond. Only computers are capable of managing battles in interstellar space.

This is not to say that the human element would never be present in space war. When faced with overwhelming odds (such as the battle with the Dominion fleet), the logical choice for the ship's computer would be not to engage the enemy. Only Sisko's determination that the Federation break the blockade compels them to attack. Despite having control of the helm and weapons, the computer is still subservient to the captain's commands. If he demands attack, the ship attacks, calculating the best possible actions under desperate measures. Perhaps the frequently used "Attack Pattern Omega" isn't a specific formation but merely a command telling the computer to fight on no matter how overwhelming the situation.

Of course, battles managed by humans are much more interesting, and the writers of *Star Trek* aren't the only ones to sacrifice believability for spectacle. Down the cineplex aisle, on a movie screen far away, *Star Wars* is no more believable.

Remember the stirring space battle scene right after the *Millennium Falcon* escapes from the *Death Star*? The fast-paced episode where Luke and Han destroy several attacking enemy fighters? We're looking at a level of technology not too different from *Star Trek*, so it's reasonable to suppose the attackers are flying at roughly impulse speed somewhere in the neighborhood of 75,000 kilometers per second. Their ray guns are firing some type of energy beam that travels at 300,000 kilometers per second. Yet Luke and Han are swinging their futuristic ack-ack guns with human reflexes, using human eyes, squeezing the triggers with fingers that operate on millisecond, not nanosecond timescales. This fight, shown at aerial dogfight speeds, could never happen in outer space.

Worse, consider the climactic attack on the Death Star. Why is Luke piloting the ship and firing the guns, instead of R2D2? The robot's reflexes are infinitely faster than the human pilot's. More to the point, exactly how long does Luke spend flying in that trench leading to the access tunnel? Some minutes, that's for sure, based on the number of conversations he has with Han Solo and Obi Wan Kenobi. The Death Star has been described as being the size of a small moon. At most it has a radius of 2,000 kilometers, giving it a maximum circumference of somewhat over 12,000 kilometers. If Luke's flying at 75,000 kilometers per second, he'd circle the Death Star six times every second. Obviously, he's traveling a lot slower. But then how does he dodge those ray cannons shooting laser beams that travel at light speed? The universe of *Star Wars* is even less logical than the universe of *Star Trek*.

Humans are always shown in control of space battles for the simple reason that people find the concept of humans being outthought or out-maneuvered by a machine distasteful. We're back to the original series' mistrust of computers, though better disguised. One of the basic mantras of this belief is that computers can't compete with humans because machines are incapable of original thought. Dare we observe that in a future of artificially intelligent computers, instantly remembering ten thousand battle scenarios might even the odds?

How close are we to this *Star Trek* future? In 1995, the Army Medical Department Center and School opened a $7.3 million-dollar Battle Simulation Center at Camp Bullis, Texas. The 13,000-square foot, high-tech facility is designed to use computer-based scenarios to teach medical staffs how to plan and carry out medical missions during major wartime campaigns. Computers simulate battlefield environments and train participants on the best ways to treat casualties and use supplies.

The Battle Simulation Center is merely one of the many projects that forms a part of the U.S. Army's Stricom Project. STRICOM stands for simulation, training and instrumentation command.

This high-tech branch of the Army is working on developing new warfighting concepts using simulation technology. One area of Stricom is devoted entirely to Inter-Vehicle Embedded Simulation Technology (INVEST) which would enable fighting vehicles and stations to use common reusable simulations components and scenarios. One of the goals of the system is to enable "direct-fire" or "line-of-sight" interactions between live and virtual systems.[1] Project STRICOM a hundred years in the future, maybe much less, and you have the battle scenarios described in this chapter.

Battles in space are going to be machine against machine. Humans aboard ship are going to be spectators, nothing more. Besides, if we take the lessons of the previous chapter to heart, it's quite probable war in space will involve one ship trying to infect its opponent with a computer virus. Why waste resources on photon torpedoes when a simple subspace transmission can cripple or destroy the enemy in milliseconds?

Artificial Intelligence

AI, or artificial intelligence, is a common term in the *Star Trek* universe. Yet it's rarely explained or even documented. In many ways it seems as much technobabble as "dilithium crystals." However, if we take a closer look at the computers of *Trek* we can deduce quite a bit about their AI abilities from the way they act.

Landru is a massive computer that has ruled Beta III for hundreds of years ("Return of the Archons," *TOS*). Landru acts to protect and preserve the culture of the world. It is self-aware and destroys what it considers threats to society, including busybody space travelers. In fact, it is so protective that it has insulated the planet from all outside influences or change for centuries, reducing its human population to childlike servitude.

Landru is an artificially intelligent machine. It thinks and analyzes information, but only in a very basic way. It views the world in terms of yes and no, true or false, black or white. There is no "maybe" or adaptability in its programs. The complex idea of harm has been narrowed down to the simple, linear concept of physical harm—and the opposite idea, good, has been equated

with physical safety. Landru is another anachronism blown up to gigantic speed and power, although in this case the parody is clearly intentional. It is a creation of the 1960s, when artificial intelligence was viewed primarily as the reduction of all thought processes to a series of if/then questions. This reasoning style was inadequate to deal with ambiguity or conflicting values.

Is AI the strict logic of Landru, or something entirely different?

By definition, artificial intelligence has to do with the ability of computers to think independently. Of course, the concept revolves around the basic question of how we define intelligence. Machine intelligence has always been a compromise between what we understood of our own thought processes and what we could program a machine to do.

Norbert Wiener, one of the greatest scientists of this century, was among the first to note the similarities between human thought and machine operation in the science of cybernetics that he helped found. Cybernetics is named after the Greek word for *helmsman*. Typically, a helmsman steers his ship in a fixed direction: toward a star or a point on land, or along a given compass heading. Whenever waves or wind throw the ship off this heading, the helmsman brings it back on course. This process, in which deviations result in corrections back to a set point, is called negative feedback. (The opposite, positive feedback, occurs when deviations from a set point result in further deviations. An arms race is the classic example.) The most famous example of negative feedback is a thermostat. It measures a room's temperature, then turns the heat on or off to keep the room at a desired temperature. Wiener theorized that all intelligent behavior could be traced to feedback mechanisms. Since feedback processes could be expressed as algorithms, this meant that theoretically, intelligence could be built into a machine.

This simple way of looking at human logic and applying it to machines provided a foundation for computer-science theory. Early artificial intelligence attempted to reduce our thought processes to purely logical steps and then encode the steps for use by a computer.

As noted in Chapter 1, a computer functions at its lowest level by switching between two states: binary one for TRUE, and zero for FALSE. Circuits are made from combinations of ones and zeros. This fact about circuits carried some inherent limitations: It meant that computers could calculate only through long chains of yes-no, true-false statements of the form "if A is true, go to step B; if A is false, go to step C." Statements had to be entirely true or entirely false. A statement that was 60 percent true was vastly more difficult to deal with. (When Lofti Zadeh began introducing partially true statements into computer science in the 1970s and 1980s—for example, "The sky is cloudy"—many logicians argued that this was not an allowable subject. The field of logic that deals with partially true statements is called fuzzy logic.) Ambiguity, error, and partial information were much more difficult to handle. Computers, whose original function, after all, was to compute, were much better equipped to deal with the clean, well-lighted world of mathematical calculation than with the much messier real world. It took some years before computer scientists grasped just how wide the chasm was between these worlds. Moreover, binary logic was best suited to manipulating symbols, which could always be represented as strings of ones and zeros. Geometric and spatial problems were much more difficult. And cases where a symbol could have more than one meaning provoked frequent errors.

This older school of AI is what we call the top-down approach— the heuristic IF-THEN method of applying intelligence to computers. Very methodical, very Spocklike, very much like the Emergency Holographic Medical Doctor on *Voyager*; and corresponding to the way computers think on the original series.

A breakthrough decade for top-down AI was the 1950s. Herbert Simon, who later won a Nobel Prize for economics, and Allen Newell, a physicist and mathematician, designed a top-down program called Logic Theorist. Although the program's outward goal was to produce proofs of logic theorems, its real purpose was to help the researchers figure out how people reach conclusions by making correct guesses.

Logic Theorist was a top-down method because it used decision trees; making its way down various branches until arriving at either a correct or incorrect solution.

A decision tree is a simple and very common software model. Suppose your monitor isn't displaying anything—that is, your computer screen seems to be dead. Figure 5.1 is a tiny decision tree that might help deduce the cause of the problem.

Using this approach, Logic Theorist created an original proof of a mathematical theorem, and Simon and Newell were so impressed that they tried to list the program as coauthor of a technical paper. Sadly, the AI didn't land its publishing credential. The journal in question rejected the manuscript.

In "The Changeling" (*TOS*), a top-down computer traveling through space, Nomad, beams onto the *Enterprise*. It scans a drawing of the solar system and instantly knows that Kirk and his crew are from Earth. An insane robot with artificial intelligence, Nomad mistakenly thinks that Kirk is "The Creator," its God. According to Spock, a brilliant scientist named Jackson Roykerk created Nomad, hoping to build a "perfect thinking machine, capable of independent logic." But somehow Nomad's programming changed, and the machine is destroying what it perceives to be imperfect lifeforms. Spock eventually concludes that "Nomad almost renders as a lifeform. Its reaction to emotion [like anger] is unpredictable."

In 1956, Dartmouth College in New Hampshire hosted a conference that launched AI research. It was organized by John

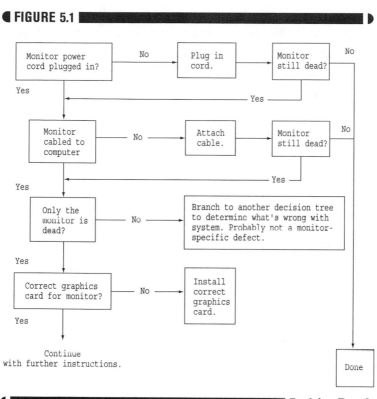

◀ **Decision Tree** ▶

Very simple decision tree that helps determine why your monitor isn't displaying anything. The real logic for the tree would be far more complex. Decision trees for expert systems—diagnostics and problem solving—are often ten or twenty pages long. One of the authors of this book wrote hundreds of pages of computer diagnostic decision trees in the 1980s. The real decision tree to diagnose a monitor malfunction was perhaps five pages long.

McCarthy, who coined the term "artificial intelligence." In addition to McCarthy, Simon, Newell, and Logic Theorist (we must list the first recognized AI program as a conference participant), the attendees included Marvin Minsky, who in 1951 with Dean Edmonds had built a neural-networking machine from vacuum tubes and *B-24* bomber parts. Their machine was called Snarc.

As far back as this 1956 conference, artificial intelligence had two definitions. One was top-down: make decisions in a yes-no, if-then, true-false manner—deduce what's wrong by elimination. The other was quite different, later to be called bottom-up: in addition to yes-no, if-then, true-false thinking, AI should also use induction and many of the subtle nuances of human thought.

The main problem with the top-down approach is that it requires an enormous database to store all the possible yes-no, if-then, true-false facts a computer would have to consider during deduction. It would take an extremely long time to search that database, and would take an extremely long time to arrive at conclusions. It would have to make its way through mazes upon mazes of logic circuits. This is not at all the way humans think. An astonishing number of thoughts blaze through the human brain all at the same time. In computer lingo, our brains are massive parallel processors.

What top-down AI brings to the table are symbolic methods of representing some of our thought processes in machines. Put more simply, top-down AI codes known human behaviors and thought patterns into computer symbols and instructions.

Perhaps the greatest boost to the top-down philosophy was the defeat of world chess champion, Gary Kasparov, by the IBM supercomputer, Deep Blue. Though not artificially intelligent, Deep Blue used a sophisticated IF-THEN program in a convincing display of machine over man.

Chess, however, is a game with a rigid set of rules. Players have no hidden moves or resources, and every piece is either on a square or not, taken or not, moveable in well-defined ways or not. There are no rules governing every situation in the real world, and we almost never have complete information. Humans use common sense, intuition, humor, and a wide range of emotions to arrive at conclusions. Love, passion, greed, anger: how do you code these into if-then statements?

A great example of top-down thinking is Data's inability to understand jokes and other human emotions. It takes Data six years to comprehend one of Geordi's jokes. When O'Brien is upset, Data asks if he wants a drink, a pillow, or some nice music. Data goes through a long list of "comfort" options, none of which makes sense to O'Brien. This is why the top-down approach is inadequate. We can't program all possibilities into a computer.

From the very beginning of AI research, there were scientists who questioned the top-down approach. Rather than trying to endow the computer with explicit rules for every conceivable situation, these researchers felt it was more logical to work AI in the other direction—to take a bottom-up approach. That is, figure out how to give a computer a foundation of intrinsic capabilities, then let it learn as a child would, on its own, groping its way through the world, making its own connections and conclusions. After all, the human brain is pretty small and doesn't weigh much, and is not endowed at birth with a massive database having full archives about the situations it will face.

Top-down AI uses inflexible rules and massive databases to draw conclusions, to "think." Bottom-up AI learns from what it does, devises its own rules, creates its own data and conclusions—it adapts and grows in knowledge based on the network environment in which it lives.

Rodney Brooks, a computer scientist at MIT, is one of bottom-up AI's strongest advocates. He believes that AI requires an intellectual springboard similar to animal evolution, that is, an artificially intelligent creature must first learn to survive and prosper in its environment before it can tackle such things as reasoning, intuition, and common sense. It took billions of years for microbes to evolve into vertebrates. It took hundreds of millions of years to move from early vertebrates to modern birds and mammals. It took only a few hundred thousand years for humans to evolve to their present condition. So the argument goes: The foundation takes forever, yet human reasoning and abstract thought take a flash of time.[1]

Therefore, current research emphasizes "survival" skills such as robotic mobility and vision. Robots must have visual sensors and rudimentary intelligence to avoid obstacles and to lift and sort objects.

How are the two approaches different? Captain Kirk, searching desperately for clues to a murder, instructs the ship's computer to identify similar crimes taking place on other planets over the course of the past several hundred years. Meanwhile, Jack the Ripper's essence invades the ship's computer and takes control. Spock issues a "class A compulsory directive" to the computer, instructing it to "compute to the last digit, the value of pi." The computer churns and grinds, doing nothing but calculating the infinite value of pi ("Wolf in the Fold," *TOS*). Both actions, searching a huge database for a limited set of attributes as well as devoting its entire processing capability to calculating a linear sequence of numbers, mark this as a top-down machine.

Some years later, the *Enterprise-D* is caught in an asteroid field by a booby-trapped derelict spaceship. Any use of the *Enterprise* engines is dangerous. Geordi has the computer call up a simulation of Dr. Lea Brahms, who designed the starship's propulsion unit. Within a short time, Geordi and Lea are working together to solve the problem that threatens the crew's existence ("Booby Trap," *TNG*). The Lea simulation actually reasons and reaches conclusions about a novel situation, much as a human would do. The simulation is so human-like that Geordi grows quite attached to it, causing himself considerable embarrassment when the real Lea Brahms shows up a few months later.

In the original series, the computers were all top-down machines. That was the generally accepted theory during the filming of the show. By the time of *The Next Generation*, bottom-up AI had become widely accepted. Thus the *Enterprise-D* computer seems much more capable than its predecessor. But perhaps not capable enough.

A great deal of the *Star Trek* universe revolves around the concept of artificial intelligence. Without it, the computers of the twenty-fourth century wouldn't be that much different from what we have today. The ship's computer wouldn't be able to answer questions, replicators and transporters wouldn't work, and Data wouldn't be nearly as interesting. Nor would Johnny Fontaine be able to give Odo advice about women.

Let's take a more specific look at the similarities and differences between the human brain and the computer. This will give us a basis for analyzing Data, the holosuites and holodecks, Professor Moriarty, and other facets of bottom-up AI in *Star Trek*.

First the similarities:

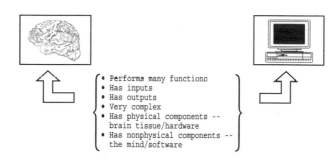

```
• Performs many functions
• Has inputs
• Has outputs
• Very complex
• Has physical components --
  brain tissue/hardware
• Has nonphysical components --
  the mind/software
```

The brain and the computer have some obvious things in common. The brain simultaneously daydreams, calculates overdue invoices that customers haven't paid, wonders if it's in love, wonders when the lunch guest will finally arrive at the office or whether the guest is lost, worries about Mom, and so forth. The computer simultaneously prints a chapter of this book, saves the chapter in case the power blows, downloads a file from the Internet, calculates overdue invoices that customers haven't paid, and so forth.

Similar, and yet different. The brain daydreams, creates, and worries; the computer does none of those things.

The brain accepts inputs from the eyes, skin, and blood. The computer accepts inputs from the keyboard, voice instructions, and data feeds. The brain issues output to the eyes, skin, and blood; the computer to the screen, networking cables, data feeds.

Both are very complex. Both have components of hardware and software, though of different materials and composition. But although we can build a working computer, we can't build a human brain. Despite their similarities the two are very different.

The basic circuitry in computers relies on the TRUE-FALSE, ON-OFF popping of micro-switches. Neurons in our brain also have TRUE-FALSE, ON-OFF states: excited and inhibited. When the voltage across a membrane rises sharply, the neuron is excited and releases chemicals (neurotransmitters) that latch onto receptors of other neurons. When the voltage drops sharply, the neuron is inhibited. Seems awfully similar to the binary ON-OFF states of the digital computer, doesn't it?

But if we look more closely at neural processes, we see a huge difference. Neurons actually behave in an analog rather than a digital manner.* Events leading to neural excitement build up, as

_____

*A digital signal has two discrete voltage levels. An analog signal varies continuously between minimum and maximum voltages.

if climbing a hill—this is a feature of analog signals. In addition, ions may cross the cell membrane even if neurotransmitters aren't received, and these ions may excite the neuron anyway. Sometimes, a neuron oscillates between intense and minor excitement levels without any outside stimulation. The more a neuron excites itself, the more prone it will be to outside stimulation.

In a computer, the shape of the motherboard—large rectangle, small rectangle, oblong, oval (we've never seen an oblong or oval motherboard, but it's an interesting concept)—has no effect on how the computer functions. Positioning components close together, shortening circuit travel, and the choice of the actual components: these conditions certainly affect the processing speed and power of the computer. However, most motherboards are rectangles, and the actual shape really doesn't have some radical influence, such as popping an ON to OFF or making a NOR into an XOR.

The neuron, however, is quite different. There are approximately fifty neuron shapes that can change the state of the neuron from excited to inhibited, or vice-versa. For example, an incoming signal becomes weaker as it traverses a really long dendrite to the neuron body. A signal that travels along a short dendrite will be much more powerful when it hits the neuron body. In addition, it takes a higher dose of neurotransmitter to excite a fat neuron than to excite a small one.

Also, the brain uses a finite set of neurons to perform a flexible number of tasks in parallel. Neurons may interact in overlapping, multiple networks within the brain; a single neuron simultaneously communicates with many others in many neural networks. And by intercommunicating constantly across these multiple networks, neurons learn to adapt and respond to their environments. We liken the brain to a muscle: the more you use it, the stronger it becomes.

The more you do trigonometry problems, for example, the better you'll be at them twenty years from now.[*]

How do we build such properties into a computer?

The ultimate result of bottom-up AI is what we think of as "alife," literally artificial life. In this type of computer intelligence, digital organisms (entities, nodes, or units) not only adapt to their environment but reproduce, feed, and compete for resources. Their offspring evolve naturally over generations to become increasingly suited to their environments. Remember the nanite episode ("Evolution") of *The Next Generation,* in which microscopic computer creatures infiltrated the ship? It isn't really that farfetched. Such digital creatures exist today in prototype form.

Some alife creatures use genetic algorithms that affect their life expectancy. The creatures have genomes to define what they're like, how they act, what they do. To reproduce, alife creatures cross-breed, and sometimes, as with biological life, the genomes are accidentally mutated, creating a next digital generation that is quite different from its parents.[†]

Some alife creatures grow through what might be thought of as digital embryonics. Such a creature exists in silicon, which is di-

---

[*]Actually, if you think trig is fun when you first learn it, you'll probably remember trig forever. It's not practice that makes us perfect, it's enjoyment. This factor makes us wonder how our neural pathways are really strengthened. If we like a particular subject—say, organic chemistry—we tend to remember the material easily without intense study and repetition. So how do our neural pathways strengthen and become accustomed to excitement patterns? And how could we possibly reproduce such an occurrence (such as feeling that organic chemistry is fun but calculus is not) in a creature such as Data?

[†]In our near-future technothriller *The Termination Node* (Del Rey Books, January 1999), genetically constructed digital alife creatures steal fifty billion dollars through the Internet.

vided into cells—where a row and column intersect as on a sheet of graph paper. Each cell contains a genome that's defined in random access memory. At the beginning of its life, the creature is the only individual in the silicon environment. This organism has a certain number of cells, just as we do at birth. Each cell has a special function, though the creature can have many cells that do the same thing. (For example, we have many skin cells and many nerve cells.) Which genes of the digital organism's cell will be functional depends on a cell's row and column—its location—in the creature.

When the alife world begins, only one cell contains the entire genome of the organism. The first cell divides, just as it would in a biological embryo. Now there are two digital cells that each contain the entire genome of the organism. Soon, the entire digital creature exists, born digitally in a manner based on biology. By combining digital embryonics with evolutionary algorithms, we have the potential to grow truly complex, novel alife environments.

Aside from Wesley Crusher's experiment that swamped the *Enterprise* with nanites ("Evolution," *TNG*), *Star Trek* features only a few alife creatures. For example, the exocomp servomechanisms on planet Tyrus VIIA, which Data protects at risk to his own life when he realizes that they have achieved self-awareness, were created by an evolutionary process ("The Quality of Life," *TNG*). But *Star Trek* characters such as Data and Lea Brahms clearly are not alife. For example, they don't possess such features as cellular division and reproduction. They did not evolve.

More common than alife is the simple form of AI built into today's robots. Back in 1969, a robot named Shakey was able to move around seven rooms that contained obstacles made of varying geometric shapes. Shakey received commands—such as

"Bring me a box"—from a computer console. Then he* rode around on his little wheels, scooted past the obstacles, snaked through the rooms, scooped up a box, and returned it to some central location.

The authors dream about going to MIT to play with the robots. We've read of insect robots, and even more cool, robots that wander around the laboratories and annoy people. Just reading about these robots makes us drool. Herbert the robot is extremely Borg-like. He steals stuff from the office of the MIT professors. He has twenty-four microprocessors, thirty infrared sensors, a hand to pick stuff up, an arm, and an astonishing optical system. Then there's the six-legged giant insect called Genghis, propelled by twelve motors, maneuvering around the halls using twelve force sensors, six heat sensors, and two sensory whiskers(!). At MIT and other universities, there are many other Borglike robots wandering around already. Research is underway to construct robots with dual arms, plus speech and hearing skills. This is an intensely exciting part of modern life. We'll return to some of these issues, and others (such as vision in an android) in the chapter dealing with Data.

For now, let's return to the issue of artificial intelligence. Let's have some fun. We'll consider several idle thoughts and how a top-down AI would react compared to a bottom-up AI (see Table 5.1).

As you can see, logic doesn't necessarily produce correct answers. People infer things, and we make mistakes. Logic yields

---

*We can't think of Shakey as an "it" any more than we can think of Data as an "it." A bias of computer people, perhaps. The monster machine on which this chapter's being typed began its shaky life as a "he," a computer version of Frankenstein (with Wolfie, based on The Wolfman, sitting by the opposite wall). As the monster calmed down and behaved in a more appropriate manner, it somehow became a "she." Go figure.

conclusions based on premises that we assume are true. However, if the premises are false, then the conclusions are false. Data's sometimes distressing dealings with human behavior clearly show that linear logic isn't always correct. Mr. Spock discovered the same truth years before Data.

Perhaps the most astonishing artificially intelligent creatures in the *Star Trek* universe are the living holograms. Dr. Moriarty ("Elementary, Dear Data," "Ship in a Bottle," *TNG*) is the result of the ship's computer trying to come up with a villain smarter than Data. Though he never achieves independence from the holodeck, Moriarty still appears to have achieved sentience. Even more interesting are the inhabitants of Yadera II, an entire village consisting of holographic images so sophisticated that they think themselves normal beings ("Shadowplay," *DS9*). Odo and Dax repair the holographic generator on the planet so that life can continue without interruption.

There's no question that AI exists in the *Trek* future. Yet in some ways the AI of 300 years from now seems extremely primitive. Why doesn't the computer on the *Enterprise* talk directly to the crew? Why does anyone need to tap a communicator badge? When Captain Picard is on the holodeck and a message arrives for him from Starfleet command, why doesn't the computer tell him directly about the transmission? When Geordi or Rom needs to repair some damage inside a Jeffries tube, why doesn't the computer give him instructions (much as Spock tells Dr. McCoy how to reconnect his brain in the classic adventure ("Spock's Brain," *TOS*)? Better still, why doesn't the computer simply make the repairs itself? When the Kazon attack *Voyager*, why doesn't the ship's computer, filled with ten thousand attack scenarios, give Captain Janeway some advice on what to do?

We suspect the creators of *Star Trek* may have felt that making the computer too powerful might worry their audience. Just as

● TABLE 5.1

Humanoid Thought	Top-Down Intelligence	Bottom-Up Intelligence
I remember when I was three years old and Dad wore that floppy felt hat every time we went fishing. He'd pull the hat over his eyes, bloat his cheeks and make sucking noises. Mom would say, "Dad, can't you ever be an adult?" My friends and I would laugh with Dad and bloat our cheeks, too.	Anyone who pulls a floppy felt hat over his eyes may not be an adult. Anyone who bloats his cheeks may not be an adult. Anyone who makes sucking noises may not be an adult. Any one of the above three conditions suffices to prove that a person may not be an adult. The humanoid's father was not an adult.	Why does she remember sucking noises and bloated cheeks with such fondness? Why did she and her friends laugh and bloat their cheeks, too? Is it a warm and personal thing to make sucking noises and bloat your cheeks? Does it imply emotion? I sure wish that I could feel emotions such as the humanoid remembering her Dad. I will ask the humanoid to tell me more about her memories so I can learn how humans feel these warm emotions for each other.
If I can somehow get a holographic simulation of a girl writhing naked on a bed, I'll make lots of money.	A holographic simulation of a girl writhing naked on a bed is worth a lot of money. A holographic simulation of a girl writhing in clothes on a bed may not be worth anything, or may be worth some variable amount of money. A holographic simulation of a girl lying still but naked on a bed may not be worth anything, or may be worth some variable amount of money.	It is not appropriate to make a holographic simulation of anyone without his or her permission. The humanoid is doing something wrong.

A holographic simulation of a girl sitting on a bed (or partially draped on the bed, etc.) but naked may not be worth anything, or may be worth some variable amount of money.

A holographic simulation of someone other than the girl, whether that person is clothed or naked, may or may not be worth some amount of money.

(etc., etc., etc.)

Strong muscles imply that a person has honor. If a person has honor, it implies that the person must "work out" on the holodeck.

What does "work out" mean:

(a) Perform his usual main bridge duties?
(b) Exercise his muscles?
(c) Celebrate the status of having honor?

And if so, how does one celebrate on the holodeck?

(etc., etc., etc.)

The humanoid works out a lot in the holodeck. He has strong muscles. This gives him a feeling of honor. I know this from past experience with the humanoid.

My muscles are strong!
I have honor!
I must go work out in the holodeck.

with space battles and space navigation, people prefer to think that they, not machines, are still in charge. After all, it's only a small step from AI to some equivalent of Kirk's computer nemesis, Landru, controlling a world—in ways that are more sophisticated but no less insidious. In the real future, three centuries from now, we suspect that the computers will be running the starships, and the crew, if present at all, will be merely along for the ride. This is a vision of space travel totally rejected by *Star Trek*.

Data

In "Inheritance" (*TNG*), the *Enterprise-D* travels to the Altrean star system to help scientists infuse energy into an unstable planet core. (What? Never mind. We're computer scientists, not geophysicists.) While working on the project, Data meets Dr. Juliana Tainer, who reveals that she was once married to Noonien Soong, Data's creator. Having worked with Soong on Data's creation; Tainer is in effect his mother.

Data initially is suspicious of Tainer, but eventually he believes her story. She knows too much about his past and how he was created. Yet when they perform together in a concert, Data's suspicions increase.

What makes Data suspicious of Tainer? She plays her piece in the concert perfectly. Exactly the same as when they practiced earlier. No human musician, no matter how well trained, is capable of duplicating a performance note for note, nuance for nuance. Dr. Tainer performs with precise pitch and intonation. Only a robot or android can achieve such exactness.

In addition, no two musicians play identical renditions of a classical piece. Interpretations vary widely, depending on a performer's personality, state of mind, and physical health, as well as the influences of specific teachers. An excellent musician does far

Data

more than play the right notes at the right speed. Data deduces that Dr. Tainer is an android because she performs as he does on his violin, with absolute precision and absolutely no human substance. In a sense, music is one of the things that makes Data more and less than human.

Data is perhaps the most fascinating creation in the entire *Star Trek* universe. We know more about him than just about any other character featured in the shows. In the best tradition of science fiction, Data's adventures explore what it means to be human. In addition, Data provides an excellent look at the future of artificial intelligence and robotics research.

Data is a far cry from the human-dominating androids of the Kirk episodes. Despite his stereotypical android mannerisms*, he has very human qualities, all of them positive. He's kinder than almost anyone we know. He's gentle and sweet, decisive and firm. He doesn't lie. He's one of the most lovable characters from any *Trek* series. It's easy to understand why Geordi considers Data his best friend. If the computers of the original series were all either stupid and servile or controlling and dangerous, Data represents a departure: a genuinely utopian vision of the ideal computer. He's extraordinarily powerful yet completely unthreatening. That the show's creators can invent a Data, and the audience can embrace him, says a great deal about how much our views of computers have changed in a generation.

---

*According to traditional science fiction, Data isn't really an android but a sentient robot. Androids are generally considered to be artificial biological beings created in growth vats, much like clones. A number of 1950s science fiction novels deal with the dilemma of whether androids deserve to be considered human. The late SF writer Philip K. Dick used the terms android and robot interchangeably, and the scriptwriters of *TNG* seem to have followed his lead.

Is Data possible based on research being done right now? Will he be possible in fifty years? Three hundred? Or is Data pure television, a creation mirroring our hopes and dreams, but physically impossible?

Since we're considering perhaps the most complex single machine in the entire Federation, the answer is also complicated.

In "Inheritance," Data plays a violin. This is not an activity we normally associate with artificial beings. Still, we've seen Data's hands move across the computer keyboard with inhuman speed. While no one's comparing typing with playing a violin, the motor skills involved are quite similar. Both require precise finger movements in a specific order. Though moving a bow requires hand and arm coordination as well, Data often types with one hand while doing other tasks at the same time. He enters commands into the keyboard with the same exactness with which he plays the violin. Both operations require skill, but neither depend on emotions.

Data, who constantly strives to appear human, expresses various emotions on his face as he plays the violin. But these expressions are no more than animatronic reactions designed specifically to appeal to his audience. As an android, he's incapable of playing with spontaneity and feeling.

A machine playing a musical instrument? Impossible—unless you've listened to player pianos, mechanized violins, or orchestrions; specialized devices built to duplicate the motions made by human operators using such instruments. Still, they're a far cry from Data bowing a Prokofiev violin sonata.

Data needs fingers capable of the most delicate, sophisticated motions made by any human. Fortunately, being robotic, once he performs the task a single time, he can duplicate it, following the exact sequence of actions. Once taught a sequence of dance steps, Data performs them perfectly from then on. His only problem is modifying the routine or creating a new pattern. The same applies to painting. He can perfectly copy numerous masterpieces but creating his own composition is a much more difficult task. While creating mechanical fingers capable of such precise movement seems impossible, it's not dream stuff. We're already entering the robotic age.

Robots have been used in factory assembly lines for years. One difference between them and their science-fiction counterparts is that real robots don't look like people. There's no reason for them to have two arms and two legs. Built to perform specific jobs, they often use multiple arms, are firmly rooted to the factory floor, and use a variety of heat and magnetic scanners.

NASA has been one of the leading developers of robots during the past few decades. It's a lot cheaper and safer to send robots on long space missions than humans. Instead of a manned flight to Mars, which would have taken decades to prepare and launch, we had *Sojourner*, the *Mars Pathfinder* robot, walking across the sands of the red planet. An interesting aspect of *Sojourner* was its use of shape-memory alloys to perform certain scientific experiments. These unique metals exhibit large changes in shape when heated or chilled. In *Sojourner*, SMAs created motion. Invented by Geoffrey Landis and Phillip Jenkins of NASA, SMAs rely on Flexinol "Muscle Wire" (1.2-inches long by .006-inches thick, with a breaking strength stronger than stainless steel) to provide a force capable of lifting over 11 ounces.[1]

Three hundred years from now, an advanced form of "muscle wire" could allow Data's body to operate with flawless perfection. Most likely, Data's version of muscle wire will be made from microscopic components. In a world of nanotechnology, invisible computers will create invisible gears, levers, cables, and beams that perform instructions issued by invisible processors.

For example, here's a possible scenario. Data's positronic brain* executes the stored routine for a favorite concerto. The routine issues commands to his nanotechnology gears and levers—the invisible components that make his arms and fingers move. A command to play a B-flat results in his left finger pressing the violin string at the B-flat position and his right arm moving the bow across the correct string. This is the kind of thing we see in "Inheritance."

Think of Data as an advanced form of digital music player. There will be no need for an android in three hundred years to move a bow across a violin string. He can simply emit the music digitally, with all human interpretation built into his rendition. Indeed, he'll be able to play multiple renditions of the same piece, and even interpret a new piece as if he were a famous human musician. An android as sophisticated as Data will go even further in technique than the best human violinist. He'll be able to merge the styles of the finest human violinists and emit music that reaches new heights.

Perhaps Data's fingers will move on the instrument and perhaps his right arm will move the bow, but we doubt it. The only reason for these fake movements by an android is for show, that is, to fool a human audience into believing that the android is playing the violin. The crew knows that Data is an android, and there's no way to fool them into believing that he's anything else.

Like other facets of *Star Trek*, Data's technology represents part of what's happening today but doesn't make the leap to tomorrow.

The robots that helped clean Three Mile Island were not the least bit humanoid, but they performed tasks impossible for hu-

---

*The term *positronic brain* is a tribute to Isaac Asimov, who first used the term in a series of short stories about robots written in the early 1940s. Asimov freely admitted in numerous interviews that he used the term *positronic* because it sounded good.

Data

mans. Strangely enough, such servo machines are nearly nonexistent on *Star Trek*. Humans do all the dangerous work. Data is the only functioning robot, and except for his odd skin color and somewhat unusual notions, he could be mistaken for a man.

The technology used by NASA and other robot manufacturers is already filtering into everyday life. Super micro, remote control servo motors are available to independent robot makers for constructing robotic hands with dexterous fingers. These same servo motors allow experimenters to build small walking robots. Hobbyists can buy mini-serial-servo controllers that handle 64 remote control servos at one time. The software associated with the controllers is easily linked to a computer and, depending on disk space, can record and program billions of moves. If run by a positronic brain with unlimited storage and FTL processing (we take these elements as givens, though as noted in Chapter 2, they're somewhat ludicrous), that's more than enough motions for Data to play the violin flawlessly or do just about any other task.

Even the simplest human action, such as walking, turning, or holding a pencil, requires the coordinated effort of hundreds of muscles and reflexes, all controlled by the brain. More complex tasks need thousands of actions. Creating a robot capable of duplicating human activity once seemed an unattainable goal. But with the incredible leaps in computer memory and CPU speed, what once appeared impossible is fast becoming probable.

Data can produce twenty-three paintings in six hours and twenty-seven minutes. He uses both hands, one brush in each, to create two paintings at a time ("Birthright, Part 1," *TNG*). He simultaneously listens to and absorbs more than one hundred and fifty classical music compositions ("A Matter of Time," *TNG*). Using "the Fourier system," his eyes appear to have random blinking patterns.

Data's body resembles that of an adult human male. As we learn in "The Most Toys" and "Disaster," it's composed primarily of nonconductive tripolymer composites and molybdenum-cobalt alloys. Combining this nearly indestructible skeleton with powerful microscopic motors and a muscular system using "muscle wire" makes him incredibly strong; in "Power Play" (*TNG*), Data puts one hand around Captain Picard's neck and lifts him completely off the floor. He exhibits similar feats of strength in a number of *Next Generation* adventures. Still, why doesn't he use his strength to help his human shipmates more often? Perhaps only for aesthetic reasons: the special effects involved might look too corny.

Data contains a functioning respiratory system, though he has no need to breathe. He uses it primarily for thermal regulation ("Brothers" and "Birthright, Part 1," *TNG*), implying that it serves as his system fan. Indeed, Data claims that he can function for extended periods inside a vacuum. Yet Data seems to breathe like any ordinary human—his nose isn't huge, he doesn't suck large amounts of air into his mouth or through his ears. When he's in very hot environments, the amount of air brought into his body through his nostrils probably wouldn't suffice to keep him cool. A sophisticated computer today requires steady, cool temperatures to function without system error. If you have a machine with multiple processors and powerful disk drives, you need fan ammunition inside your tower. Data's brain is more than a multiple processor, and his body contains unknown yet advanced equipment: certainly, Data requires a highly controlled system temperature.

He does indicate, in "Disaster" (*TNG*), that a power surge of half a million amps would cause a system failure in his internal processors and a meltdown of his primary power couplings. Half a million amps is a huge amount of current.

The word amp is short for amperes, which is the number of electrons moving past a point within one second. One ampere of current implies the flow of 6,243 quadrillion electrons per second. Force, which is measured in volts, is the pressure difference between two points. Without a pressure difference in a circuit, current doesn't flow. Here's a very simplified view of this idea:

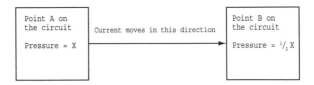

Think of the current as air. Think of the two points on the circuit as two tires. Think of the arrow as a hose. Clearly, if one tire (Point A) has twice as much pressure as the other tire (Point B), the air in the hose flows from the first tire into the second tire. Air flows until the pressure in both tires is equal.

Current is the same. It moves from the circuitry point with more pressure to the circuitry point with less pressure. One volt forces one amp of current through one ohm of resistance. (Resistance opposes the flow of current/electrons.) In 1827, Dr. Georg Simon Ohm defined what became known as Ohm's Law: The amount of current in a circuit is directly proportional to the voltage applied to the circuit and inversely proportional to the resistance. In addition, we have Watt's Law: The power (as measured in watts) in a circuit equals the current (amperes) multiplied by the voltage (ohms). If, for example, we have a 150-watt light bulb drawing 1.5 amps, then we require 100 volts.

Now let's try to determine how much current is implied by half a million amps, the amount that melts Data. We don't know Data's resistance, only that his positronic brain has "several layers of shielding to protect [him] from power surges." The average computer today might use 5 or 3.3 volts. Voltages in computer systems are shrinking. We're told that Data runs on "microhydraulic power." Either he uses microvolts (10^{-6}) or nanovolts (10^{-9}).

Because Data's built from nanocircuits, he probably requires nanovolt components. To keep things simple for now, let's assume that when we add up all the resistance in Data, we have a full 1 volt. Remember that our 150-watt light bulb uses 100 volts. Let's apply the numbers to the algorithm:

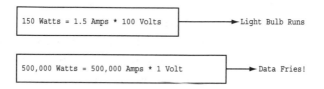

So based on our 150-watt light bulb, we figure that Data short circuits if we apply power roughly equal to that of 3,333.33 ordinary 150-watt light bulbs (500,000 / 150 = 3,333.33 light bulbs). Data supposedly fries at 500,000 watts. The typical person might generate a few hundred watts just typing a Data chapter on the keyboard. The human brain consumes approximately the energy of an ordinary light bulb.

Something is wrong with our assumption about the 1 volt. We must move to micro or nanovolts to reduce the amount of energy Data needs and generates. At 1 microvolt, Data would generate 500 watts, which is closer to the human body.

Still, it's puzzling. It seems that Data would have a total system meltdown long before the current hit half a million amps. And if he somehow runs on close to half a million amps, he must glow in the dark; or as our friend Bill Tate says, "Data must have one heck of a glowing personality."

These are very crude guesses, of course. We'd like to know how much power Data generates autonomously to run himself. And given that Data has only some undefined shielding to protect his positronic brain and only breathing as an internal cooling system, how does he withstand power surges of more practical amounts, such as any number below 500,000 amps?

Perhaps Data does generate 500 watts of power using a total of 1 microvolt of pressure. Perhaps it requires four cooling-fan noses to keep his system from shutting down. Perhaps he needs giant nostrils to suck in the air to keep his legs from turning off during system overheating. If he has giant nostrils, though, nano-tech diseases could enter and destroy him. Not good.

Data's system cooling probably will occur through skin pores, not nostrils; but we must take his nostrils and lungs as concrete system designs. His humanoid composition is a given of *Star Trek*.

We're told that Data's circulatory system distributes biochemical lubricants throughout his body. But we don't know what the lubricants are or what they do. We can only assume that they somehow oil his parts. Perhaps they are released periodically by nanomachines in Data's body. But what if the nanomachines are off slightly? Would the lubricants slosh throughout Data's internals, causing major system damage? He hasn't any method to repair himself aside from running internal diagnostics of his positronic brain. Even Geordi, who knows better than anyone else how to repair Data, would surely be clueless when it comes to a catastrophe such as an over-internal-lubrication job by some malfunctioning nano-equipment. Geordi uses large wrenches to repair Data, not nanosurgical devices.

Besides, why does Data require biochemical lubricants? What does the bio aspect bring to the mix? Data comments that he rarely needs the services of Dr. Crusher ("Data's Day," *TNG*), which implies that sometimes he does need medical help. In what cases, and under what conditions, does Dr. Crusher service Data? These are things that we'd love to see explored in future *Star Trek* movies.

According to Data, his circulatory system regulates his micro-hydraulic power and provides him with a human pulse. We're clueless why Data needs a pulse. If it's solely to make him fit into human crowds without being noticed, then why is his skin greenish? We'd notice a man with green skin more quickly than we'd feel his pulse.* Yet Data claims that nobody has ever asked him if his hair grows, and indeed, nobody's ever noticed that he breathes. What were those computer scientists doing when they first found Data and sent him to Starfleet Academy? Didn't they notice that the only android in existence breathes and regulates the growth of his own hair? Or that he has a pulse?

While it's clear that a machine like Data can't be constructed today, if the science of robotics continues to advance at the speed of general computer technology, then creating a robot like Data should be possible within the next century or two. But as more than one mad scientist in old SF movies has learned to his despair, creating the body isn't enough. It's the brain that matters.

In *Star Trek*, mankind's greatest scientists have been unable to produce functioning androids for hundreds of years. They have one amazing android called Data, but they don't understand the technology that created him. We're asked to believe that the reclusive Dr. Noonien Soong was the only scientist who ever perfected a positronic brain. That no other cybernetist among the many billions of inhabitants of the Federation has ever been able

---

*Oddly enough, when Data's "mother" visits him, nobody notices that she's also an android. Even Data is fooled for a long time. Unlike Data, his android mother has a feedback processor that sends out a false biosignal, fooling everyone into believing she's human. Even more strange is that she never knew she was an android. Soong designed her to shut down if she ever learned the truth.

Data

to duplicate his work. And that androids other than Data don't exist.[*]

In "Inheritance," Juliana Tainer says that Data is the fifth android built by Dr. Soong.[†] The first three artificial beings were total or partial failures. The fourth was named Lore, but he was taken apart by Dr. Soong when he exhibited strong antisocial behavior ("Brothers," *TNG*). Since creating an android body three centuries from now doesn't appear to be an insolvable task, the problem obviously was in their brains.

In "The Offspring," Data builds another android like himself. This new android, whom Data considers his child, is named Lal and is similar to Data but in some ways more advanced. Still, her positronic brain fails and she dies. Not even Data seems to know exactly how his mind works.

In "Evolution" (*TNG*), Captain Picard permits an alien intelligence to enter Data's brain. Apparently, it's simple for the alien nanites to figure out exactly how Data's brain operates. As Data tells Picard, "I can easily furnish the nanites with the schematic design of my neurological structure. Entering my neural net would require no more than their most basic skills." It's odd that a microscopic alien intelligence can penetrate, understand, and

---

[*]In the original series, Kirk and crew encounter androids in such adventures as "What Are Little Girls Made Of?" and "I, Mudd." But these androids are always the results of alien super-science, and they lack independent intelligence. They are robotic drones, controlled by central computers. "To function as they do," Spock tells us, "each android mind must be one component of a mass brain linked to a central locus." In the Kirk episodes, of course, the androids have perfect human female anatomy and wear harem-type outfits. They obey male orders and often express fascination when Captain Kirk attempts to seduce them.

[†]All the androids, except of course Juliana, were built in Dr. Soong's image.

use Data's brain instantly, whereas neither human scientists nor Data can reproduce it.*

It's pretty clear that all of Data's knowledge is in his skull, and not dispersed throughout his body, even though that would make more sense. Geordi often opens Data's head, never, for instance, his stomach to fiddle with his positronic net, his "brain." Nor does Data seem to have the same redundancy that's built into the ship's computer. When his head's gone, he's inoperable ("Time's Arrow," *TNG*).

Data is more than a mere computer walking about in an artificial humanoid body. As an android, he is more than a machine, though less than human. This fact is demonstrated quite clearly in "The Schizoid Man." In that adventure, Data meets Dr. Ira Graves, who was Dr. Soong's mentor. In a sense, Graves is Data's grandfather. Unfortunately, when the two meet, Graves is dying. He deactivates Data and transfers his mind into Data's positronic brain. Though Data has no capacity for emotion (this is before he retrieved the emotion chip from Lore), Graves in Data's mind exhibits a full sweep of emotions, ranging from love to anger. Picard and Graves/Data get involved in a philosophical argument about whether Data, technically a machine, has the right to exist if it means Graves will die. Later, when Graves transfers his mind into the ship's computer, there's no evidence of any emotions; the human element is gone, implying that Data's positronic brain is quite different from the *Enterprise* computer core.

---

*Data initially establishes contact with the nanites using the ship's computer. On Data's computer screen, we see the nanite's language as pink and yellow binary. It's interesting that the nanites easily penetrate Data's body, enter his "nerve circuitry," and interface with his verbal program—that is, speak English through Data's lips. Amazing! And certainly in return for the gift of an entire planet on which to live and flourish, we'd think the nanites might easily be persuaded to give Data the blueprints of his own brain.

According to Data, his brain possesses a storage capacity of 100,000 terabytes of memory, or 10^{17} bytes. He also states that his positronic brain processes 60 trillion computations per second. Checking back to Chapter 2, we note that Data thus has enough memory to hold 1,000 Libraries of Congress. It's not close to the memory capacity of the *Enterprise*, but it's still a lot of memory. When Geordi and Data discuss letting Data run some ship subroutines through his brain, it's not that unbelievable ("A Fistful of Datas," *TNG*). Except perhaps for the subroutines they test—weapons systems, for example, not a prime choice.

Many scientists feel the human brain has a maximum memory capacity of three terabits. Which would mean Data has the memory storage of more than a quarter-million people. With that much memory, there's plenty of room for subroutines to coordinate all the necessary movements Data needs to handle such activities as walking, talking, even playing the violin. But all that knowledge can't make him creative. He still has to be taught what to do before he can do it. While Data's positronic brain can process 60 trillion computations per second, it's estimated that the human brain can process 10 trillion bytes per second. He thinks faster than people, but not that much faster.

Data's positronic brain is supposed to be a neural network with lots of parallel processing. Let's try to figure out what this means.

We talked a little about neurology and artificial intelligence in Chapter 5. The human brain contains approximately 100 billion to 200 billion neurons that fire about 10 million billion times per second.* Each neuron connects to roughly 10 thousand other

---

*Estimates vary about the number of neurons in our brain. But we have a lot. A slug brain, by contrast, has approximately 20,000 neurons, yet is a sufficiently interesting neural net for major computer-science research studies.

neurons. This is how the brain handles trillions of operations per second. It's an extremely complex neural network.

A computer-neural network is a simplified version of a biological neural network. In the biological form, a neuron accepts input from its dendrites and supplies output to other neurons through its axons. The neuron applies weights to the connections, or synapses, between dendrites and axons. A higher weight might be applied to a synapse related to touching fire than to a synapse about seeing the pretty color of fireball orange.

In the computerized version, each "input neuron" feeds information into every neuron in what is called the hidden layer, which may have one or multiple layers of neurons. If the hidden layer has two layers of neurons, for example, then every neuron in the first hidden layer feeds into every neuron in the second. Every neuron in the last hidden layer feeds into neurons in the output layer.

The designer of a neural net provides different weights for the connections among neurons. While our brain receives input from many sources, such as sensations on our skin, what we hear, what we smell, and so forth, an artificial neural network takes input only from values we provide, and then it weighs everything and supplies a best-guess answer. We know, for example, that 1.00 + 1.00 equals 2.00. An artificial-neural net may not find the problem so easy. It may guess that the answer is 1.98, or perhaps 2.04. But the artificial brain will do quite well in guessing correctly between say, a nerf football and a soccer ball. Or even a nerf soccer ball versus a hard soccer ball. Both are spheres. Both are the same size. One is soft, the nerf; one is hard, the soccer ball.

Various methods exist for applying weights to artificial neurons, and for assembling the input, hidden, and output layers into network architectures. A neural network learns by adjusting the weights given to its neurons. A very common neural net architecture is called back propagation, which compares forecasts to actuals, then adjusts the weighted interconnections among neurons. Over time, as it compares more forecasts to actuals, the neural weights become more accurate. In a sense, the neural net itself has learned and adjusted to its environment.

The big question: is Data's positronic brain possible? It seems highly likely.

Which returns us to the question we asked early in this chapter. Would it be possible for Data to play the violin? Or bend, twist, and turn while dancing? How can a machine operate with equal or better skill than a man?

Simple. Combine microhydraulics in a body that doesn't wear out or become tired with the information storage capacity of a thousand Libraries of Congress. Mix the knowledge and motor speeds together in a control unit that processes 60 billion operations per second, and you have a dancing, fencing, walking, talking, singing, acting, typing android. It's impossible using current science, but researchers today are making tremendous strides in robotics, neural nets, and nanotechnology. Couple these strides with three more centuries of advances, and you have a humanoid robot capable of performing every physical act displayed by Data on *Star Trek*. However, Data's more than a robot. He's a sentient being. Data thinks.

Perhaps the most famous test of whether a computer is artificially intelligent was proposed by British computer scientist Alan Turing. In its simplest form, Turing stated that a computer is intelligent if it deceives a human into believing it's human. Turing's approach is a test of top-down AI.

Data has passed Turing's test many times, with inhabitants of other planets as well as his own crew. Since Data is obviously artificially intelligent with a positronic neural net, is he "top down" or "bottom up"? Or a combination of both?

Data's mind appears to be a "bottom-up" AI/neural network. He's not loaded with facts about everything in the universe (while his memory is large enough to hold the information in a thousand Libraries of Congress, it's not as huge as the one in the ship's computer). Data possesses a great deal of information. In "Birthright," *TNG*, he mentions that he's analyzed over 4,000 different religious and philosophical systems, but it is implied that this knowledge has been acquired by high-speed reading. He's shown constantly learning, growing, and evolving over a period of time. As an artificial being, Data's not shy and asks for advice and opinions, often from a long-suffering Geordi LaForge. Data has a cat named Spot and tries constantly to understand it. He even dreams and tries to learn from these dreams. Only a bottom-up creation would try to understand both romance and humor.

Data operates in the holosuite, an artificial environment, as well as the real world environment, without any problem whatsoever. ("Elementary, Dear Data," *TNG*, *Generations*, and many more episodes) Again, coping with constant novelty implies bottom-up AI neural networking.

Still, Data (along with Lore and Mrs. Soong) seems to possess vast amounts of practical and esoteric information. His mind is full of facts. Data's a great fan of Sherlock Holmes, which implies heuristic thinking and a top-down AI approach. In many *Trek* adventures, Data uses the if-then type of thinking associated with logic trees to arrive at a conclusion. More telling, to function as a highly rated Federation officer, Data must make snap decisions and do snap calculations. His mind obviously contains a huge amount of information that helps him reach these conclusions. In *Insurrection*, Data comments that if one of his legs grows, he won't be able to walk. This implies that his walking algorithms are top-down AI—they can't adapt and let Data limp. When confronted with new stimuli, Data doesn't over-react. He never

Data

breaks down. If anything, he adapts more quickly than any other crewmember ("Cause and Effect," *TNG*). His learning phase is incredibly short.

Data deals with concepts that are simple for ordinary human brains but extremely complex for artificial neural nets. What we do naturally is almost impossible to duplicate in a computer. Let's consider, for example, vision, a key issue for creating androids that interact with their environments or survive hostile situations.

The sensory abilities and neural architectures of animals tend to be based on what they need. One factor is reaction time—how long do I have to drop this chunk of meat and run before the dog sees me? Other factors are the sizes and complexities of the objects that the animal recognizes.

Human visual perception is based on much more complex input. The retina uses cells called rods to handle incoming light and cells called cones to handle incoming color. With approximately 100 million rods and cones, the retina processes images at the rate of something like 10 billion calculations per second.

After image preprocessing by the retina, the cerebral cortex takes over the image processing. Vision centers for this purpose occupy more than half of the cortex. At this point, our brain hasn't even started to determine what it is we're looking at—a ball, a field of flowers, or a crowd of people—much less fit all the objects into a moving scene, analyze who and what we know, or how we want to react. All our brain has right now is raw image data. Think of it as the collection of individual bits accumulated by a digital camera before you get to see the image, the photo, you just took.

But our visual skills are far more elaborate than the world's finest cameras. We instantly recognize and respond to textures, lights, and shades. Our brains create an imprint that is complete with texture, object boundaries, and compensation for fog, brightness, and shadow. Simply by looking at the leaves on a plant, we deduce that they are prickly, smooth, sticky, dangerous, or safe to touch. In dim or flickering light, we still recognize our friends or our enemies. Just the outline of someone's profile in heavy fog may suffice for visual recognition. We even interpret and process oddities such as optical illusions. If a satanic head appears to us in a cloud, we might conclude that—well, perhaps we need a bit more sleep.

It's unlikely that Data can process optical illusions. He might recognize Riker or Geordi from the back, he might be able to handle complex three-dimensional image processing, but he doesn't have the requisite innate human ability to process illusions or shifts in shadows and lights. His positronic neural net can learn using back propagation; in other words, by making mistakes. He might think that the satanic head in a cloud is real. For a better example, suppose the Borg, who are digitally driven creatures themselves, send Data's positronic brain some wireless visual stimulation that makes Data see all crewmembers as Borg. How would he interpret this visual information? In a dangerous situation, he might accidentally shoot Picard, thinking he's killing a Borg. Only by making a mistake—in this case a serious one—would Data learn that the Borg have impressed optical illusions into his visual system.

While Data's learning the hard way, we fear that he'd probably die. After all, he often functions under life-threatening circumstances. Is the shift of light in the corridor an alien attack or something else?

Data shows his ability to learn from his mistakes, a prime indicator of "bottom-up" artificial intelligence, in the adventure "Peak Performance." He finds himself matched in computer strategy games against an arrogant Zakdom tactician, Sima Koirami. Data loses and believes his programs must be faulty. He warns Captain Picard that his judgment might be inaccurate. He even resorts to studying his own schematics to locate the problem. It's inconceivable to him that he might lose a computer strategy game to a living being. Data's initial reactions and efforts are "top-down," as he tries to use logic-trees and "if-then" reasoning to discover why he lost. But none of his attempts bring success. It's not until he studies the problem and learns from his previous mistakes—typical "bottom-up" AI thinking—that he finally comes up with a strategy to defeat Koirami.

We can conclude that Data has "bottom-up" AI, but with more than a touch of "top-down" AI tossed in for good measure.

Androids like Data aren't just a few years away from now. We don't expect to see them strolling down the street anytime soon. Still, with the rapid developments taking place in neural nets and AI, it seems likely that beings like Data might exist well before the *Enterprise-D* ever leaves on its first mission.

In his attempt to become more human, Data's most difficult task has been to feel and understand human emotions. He has tried to understand humor ("The Outrageous Okona," *TNG*), romance ("In Theory," *TNG*), and even parenthood ("The Offspring," *TNG*). A submerged subroutine, triggered by a plasma shock, enables Data to dream. ("Birthright, Part 1," *TNG*) Originally unable to experience emotions, Data later obtained an emotion chip created by Dr. Soong and gained the ability to turn his emotions on and off ("Descent, Part 2," *TNG*, *Generations*, *First Contact*).

Apparently, the chip enables Data to feel real emotions, not computational facsimiles. When coding emotion into virtual humans, sophisticated programs may generate facial expressions and body postures that simulate emotional reactions by real people. The key word is simulate. The emotion chip does more than that for Data. It allows him to experience true emotion.

In *First Contact*, the Borg hive-queen activates Data's emotion chip and grafts a patch of organic skin onto the endoskeletal structure of Data's arm. She then blows on the skin, and Data has some kind of orgasmic upswing. A few moments later, while he is cradling the skin protectively, the Borg queen challenges him to tear it off his body. He cannot bring himself to do it. Apparently, Data's normal skin (the skin "fabric" that the nanites penetrate in "Evolution," [*TNG*]) doesn't have nerve endings that feed into his emotion chip. But his new organic skin does.

While it's clear that the movie is making a philosophical point—without an organic body, emotions aren't really possible—as a matter of simple wiring, the scene doesn't make much sense. If the internal connections between Data's normal skin and his emotion chip didn't exist before, it's hard to see how grafting a new patch of organic skin onto him could create them. Unless he has millions of unused, superfluous "nerve" endings lying just below his normal covering.

We think the movie is wrong: An organic body is not a prerequisite to emotions. Emotions are a product of evolution—a powerful adaptation that helps us learn and survive—and there's no reason why an evolved alife intelligence couldn't have them, too. Some estimates place emotional reactions in artificially intelligent computer systems by the year 2050. It all depends on how quickly the next computer revolution occurs—the one that lifts us from microprocessors to DNA, quantum, optical, holographic, and other forms of computer technology. Clearly, by Data's time, he won't require a special "emotion chip." In three or four hundred years, androids will have built-in, automatic emotional responses. The real Data will have a wide range of emotions, unlike the *Trek* Data with his static qualities of the galaxy's finest boy scout.

The Holodeck

There are many ways to relax on the *Enterprise*. People listen to music, read (one of Captain Picard's favorite activities), engage in dramatic performances, or even work up a sweat in sports. Yet without question, the holodeck is the most advanced form of entertainment ever invented.

It's on the holodeck that our favorite characters act out their most cherished dreams. The holodeck can provide an exotic background for a social gathering or settings and action for life-like interactive novels, such as the ones where Captain Picard plays the hard-boiled detective Dixon Hill. Julian Bashir plays at being an absurdly dashing secret agent, Tom Paris reinvents himself as a character in a twentieth-century science-fiction epic, and we have no doubt that the holosuite programs in Quark's library range from the romantic to the extraterrestrially revolting. Holodecks and holosuites offer a chance for relaxation, entertainment, or adventure. Unfortunately, they're also extremely unlikely to exist, even three hundred years from now.

The holodeck (we'll stick to holodecks, but everything we say about them applies equally to holosuites) relies on perhaps the most complex computer program on the *Enterprise*, as well as on transporter and replicator technology. We're told explicitly that

the holodeck is a direct outgrowth of transporter technology ("Heroes and Demons," *VGR*). Transporters, replicators, and holodecks all rely on the ability to assemble matter at the molecular level, either from a template that was disassembled elsewhere just moments before, a pattern stored in memory, or a set of general instructions. Furthermore, we're told that unlike the replicators, the holodecks create solid-seeming objects out of some sort of magnetic pseudo-particles rather than real matter. This technology clearly raises questions of plausibility, many of which are best answered by a physicist. We'll stick to computing issues.

According to the *Star Trek: The Next Generation Technical Manual*,[1] the *Enterprise* contains four main holodecks, located on Deck 11. Twenty smaller holographic units (probably similar to the holosuites in Quark's bar) are on Decks 12 and 33. The holodecks use holograms and replicator technology to create realistic and believable simulations.

The holodeck creates illusions in a variety of ways. The gridlike walls can generate images of immense distance, such as the ocean in *Generations* or the crowded vastness of a nineteenth-century London cityscape in "Elementary, My Dear Data" (*TNG*). Holograms are routinely projected onto the deck for scenery, creating everything from landscapes to ancient fortresses. Most of these background features, and the characters moving through them in non-active roles, have no need for physical form and are obviously mere projections. These effects are merely extensions of today's virtual reality programs.

What's virtual reality? It's a computer-generated world in which we move and interact with objects, other real people, and virtual reality people. It's a place that isn't really there but that offers the powerful illusion of existence.

Virtual reality today comes in two flavors. One surrounds you with three-dimensional objects and scenes so that you feel you are walking through the scenes so that you're visually surrounded by the virtual world. This effect requires equipment: virtual-reality goggles, for instance, or specially equipped rooms.

The second type of virtual reality appears before you on a two-dimensional screen, such as your computer monitor. The computer graphics and programming are so well done that a full three-dimensional world feels live on your two-dimensional screen. Many computer games are forms of virtual reality. They aren't known as virtual reality games, though, simply as three-dimensional games with some built-in artificial intelligence. Yet when we play them, we're there. Much of the basic programming for this kind of on-screen VR is the same as for the more elaborate kind. The computer doesn't care whether the virtual space it constructs is an image on a screen or a three-dimensional holographic projection.

On-screen virtual reality also exists as a result of a special programming language called the Virtual Reality Modeling Language, or VRML 2.0. Uses for interactive VRML worlds include business applications, such as walking people through the internals of equipment, showing them how to fix a machine from different angles, letting them walk though an on-line shopping store, explore battle simulations, and cruising them through the layout of a new public sports arena.

If we wanted to build a virtual world we might begin as God did, with a light source. We supply numbers defining both direction and intensity; for example:

```
DirectionalLight {
    direction    0 -0.707107 -0.707107
    intensity    0.5
    color        1 1 1
}
```

The DirectionalLight is like a stage floodlight for a virtual reality scene. It illuminates the scene with light rays parallel to the direction, a vector supplied by x, y, and z coordinates.

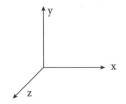

The intensity is the brightness of the light, and the color is the Red-Green-Blue (RGB) value that defines the light's color. In the RGB example of 1 1 1, each 1 represents a hexadecimal code of ff, meaning Full Red, Full Green, and Full Blue. With 1 1 1, the total color combination is white. Therefore, our light is bright white in this example.

As a caveat, you might notice that, by changing the color, intensity loses its relevance. Light emission is approximately equal to intensity times color, but with color turned to maximum white, what's the point of reducing intensity? You can just as easily reduce the color from full white to something less intense.

We might want to specify background textures or images for the ceiling (such as a sky), ground (some grass perhaps), and a wraparound world (perhaps a forest that encircles us as we move through the scenes). Or, for fast loading and easier lighting, we can just specify background colors in gradients, such as:

```
Background {
   groundAngle [ 0.9, 1.5, 1.57 ]
   groundColor [ 0 0.8 0,
                 0.174249 0.82 0.187362,
                 0.467223 0.82 0.445801,
                 0.621997 0.67 0.600279 ]
```

```
skyAngle        [ 0.1,  1.2,  1.57 ]
skyColor        [ 0.76238 0.8 0.1427,
                  0.277798 0.219779 0.7,
                  0.222549 0.390234 0.7,
                  0.60094 0.662637 0.69 ]
}
```

The groundAngle supplies a cutoff angle for each groundColor. In the example, we have four groundColor values separated by commas. Each groundColor is an RGB value, and the first (0 0.8 0) is what we might see if looking straight down. So there's one more groundColor than groundAngle.

The colors for the sky are created in the same way. One more skyColor than skyAngle, with the first skyColor the RGB value we see when looking straight up.

These are very simple examples. Rather than supply colors for the ground and sky, we can instead designate background images for the entire virtual reality scene: front, back, right, left, top, and bottom. Using this second method, we essentially define a cube of images, which together, define a panorama surrounding our virtual reality world. We can place clouds in the sky, or on the floor. We can place mountains in the distance, or on the ceiling.

At this point in coding a VR world, we have to move beyond the easy steps of defining the sky and ground. We have to create the objects that will fill the world, and we must make the objects interact and move.

To understand virtual reality code requires a basic comprehension of object-oriented programming (OOP). Way beyond the scope of this book, but to get a feeling for the holodecks—which are virtual reality worlds—we have to start somewhere.

Think of OOP as a hierarchy of objects. Each object describes a "thing," what it looks like, what it does, the data it uses. We might define various VR objects and some of the components that enable them to interact. For example, here's a snippet of code:

```
PROTO Snippet [
  exposedField SFColor  SColor 0.95 0.0121455 0.123516
  exposedField SFVec3f  SPosition  1 0 0
  exposedField SFVec3f  SSize     0.5 0.5 0.5
  field SFVec3f    activePosition 1 0 0
]
{
Transform {
  translation IS SPosition
  children [
      DEF PS PlaneSensor {
      }
      DEF box Transform {
        translation-2 0 0
        scale IS SSize
        center -2 0 0
        children [
          DEF SLight SpotLight {
            color IS SColor
            location 0 0 10
            on FALSE
          }
          Shape {
            appearance Appearance {
              material Material {
                diffuseColor IS SColor
              }
            }
```

```
             geometry Box {
                size 2.5 1 1
             }
          }
       ]
     }
  ]
}
ROUTE PS.translation_changed TO box.set_translation
DEF Sscript Script {
  url "vrmlscript:
       function SPositionCheck(pos) {
          posX = pos[0];
          activeX = activePosition[0];
       }
     "
  eventIn SFVec3f SPositionCheck
  field SFVec3f activePosition IS activePosition
}
ROUTE PS.translation_changed TO Sscript.SPositionCheck
}
```

PROTO Snippet defines an object called Snippet that we can use repeatedly in the program without consuming extra resources. Snippet itself is a simple three-dimensional brick.

Each exposedField can be accessed from other parts of the program, for example, to change the color of each Snippet we create. An exposedField implicitly knows how to handle two event types: an incoming set_ event that changes the field value, and an outgoing _changed event that sends the exposedField's changed value to another node. In the example, code can change the color, position, and size of the Snippet object.

Simple geometric constructions enable us to code the appearance of each Snippet. Thus, much of the VR world can be built up from variations on specific aspects of fundamentally identical parts.

Suppose, to make the metaphor tangible, this particular Snippet is an actual brick—or a representation of one—and you see this Snippet resting on the ground. In the VR world, you might see 45 Snippet blocks on the ground. Or 100 of them. Or only one.

Each looks likes a real brick. Each has a different color. Each feels real to your touch in the VR world. It's all programming code, it's all created from one tiny Snippet defined in VR software language.

You're immersed in this Snippet-filled VR world, just as *Trek* characters are immersed in holodeck adventures. In reality, you're sitting on a chair in your living room. But your brain's immersed in a fantasy world, the Snippet world on your computer screen (or delivered directly into your brain through your eyes via goggles).

Perhaps you pick up the brick and hurl it at a huge spider web obstructing your entrance to the cave of Dr. Cruelman. In reality, you're still sitting on a chair in your living room. Only in virtual reality are you throwing the brick at a spider web.

The PlaneSensor notices that you moved the Snippet brick. The ROUTE statements and vrmlscript enable the code to move the Snippet brick on the computer screen. It seems to you in realtime that you lifted and hurled the brick. No pause. No frame jitter. You continue to play the adventure game.

Perhaps a spider flies into the scene, angry that you destroyed its web. In the real world, spiders can't fly. In virtual reality worlds, objects and creatures can do anything we program them to do.

The VR spider might be an object composed of many parts: legs, hair, eyeballs, mouth, ears (we can do anything we want in code), a tail, and pinchers. Perhaps our VR spider has dragon-fire breath, as well. Each part of the spider can be programmed to move in any way our imagination dictates. The dragon-fire breath can spray from its tail or eyeballs. Perhaps when we throw a VR brick at the web, the spider sprays fire from whatever body part is closest to us.

In general, we can program living creatures in VR worlds to do anything we want. The only limitation is our imagination. We can code one prototype spider that defines basic parts of spiders in our VR world. From the prototype, we can then create many other spiders, each of which inherits the basic spider's properties, then adds to the mix by moving different ways, spraying bombs as well as fire, smiling sweetly and throwing flowers rather than fire, and so forth.

We route actions from one object to another. An action, such as throwing a brick at the spider web, triggers another action, such as the spider flying on scene and hurling fireballs at us.

For more complex events, the code might be done through vrmlscript, Javascript, or Java. For example, you throw the brick at the spider web, and I want my coded spider to do three actions and another spider to do four actions, plus I want these two spiders' actions to trigger an attack from six spider colonies, who live in giant webs on islands in my VR world. While I can route one event to multiple, additional events, when things get this complicated, simple routing statements may misfire during program execution. Using programming languages that offer more sophistication, when you throw that brick at the web, I can trigger complex, even artificially intelligent actions from creatures, settings, and objects anywhere in the world I've created.

Even for the twenty-fourth century, the holodeck simulations are extremely sophisticated VR programs. All the edges are perfectly done. There are no walls jutting out in the wrong place and no arches that don't close correctly. In *Trek*, the holodeck geometries never become really bizarre in either color or structure. They always maintain their real-life appearance, texture, and touch.

It might be interesting if the holosuite software offered totally imaginative worlds—places constructed like Escher drawings, for example. Today, most virtual reality and three-dimensional games are based on totally fantastic constructs.

So why don't holodecks have similar worlds? At minimum, at least during system malfunctions, Escher-type constructions and other gross abnormalities would occur. Holodeck characters wouldn't always become evil: they would disintegrate, turn into other creatures, or most likely cease to exist. Holodeck architectures could turn into holodeck characters, and vice-versa. People could go insane inside a holodeck during a system malfunction.

The technology to immerse people in virtual reality worlds began with head-mounted devices that presented three-dimensional views. Sensors picked up hand and head movements, and fed that information into software, which then altered the three-dimensional worldview for the user. Back in the late 1960s, people were already dabbling with this kind of research, though the views were only simple wireframe models.

While a wireframe shows us the corners and lines—the entire grid—of objects, more complex rendering methods show textures, patterns, colors, shine, and shadow. Wireframes today are often used to create initial three-dimensional objects, but once we're satisfied with how our model looks, we produce fully rendered final versions.

Today's virtual worlds have become so lifelike that people can become disoriented: thoroughly immersed in their virtual adventures. Still, such virtual fun often requires the user to wear headsets, hand and arm gear that looks like hospital tubes, and other special equipment. Someday these won't be necessary, but not yet.*

Ideally, immersion means that you don't know the difference between the physical world and the virtual world in which you're playing. The simultaneous perceptions of what you see and what your body feels are tightly matched. A slight disconnection throws you out of the illusion that you're in reality.

In the future, artificial intelligence combined with virtual reality will enable us to create and enter virtual worlds populated by very lifelike creatures, humans, and plants. Real people will enter these worlds and meet their inhabitants. Much as on the holodecks.

Still, there are a few logical problems with the portrayal of virtual reality holodecks in *Star Trek*.

We wonder, for example, how the ship's computer stores enough object templates for all of the world's variations and scenes on the holodecks. Every scene, every object, from a twig to an ocean ripple to a character's facial mannerisms—everything appears instantly on the holodeck from all angles, with varying lighting quality, possessing unique textures, even retaining correct dimensions at all distances. This is extraordinary virtual reality programming. Faraway objects are never hollow. They aren't in fog. They are always perfectly clear. Every eye blink, every wrinkle in every piece of clothing as characters move is consistent: Absolutely everything in the holodeck is perfectly coordinated at all times. Of course, the ship's computer has a huge amount of storage, as calculated earlier. But people in *Star Trek*

---

*There are also spectacular interactive rides at amusement parks, which rely on motion machines and synthetic actors to create an illusion of reality (such as the Star Tours ride at Disneyworld and the Jurassic Park ride at Universal Studios).

can program new adventures for the holodecks, and store and later replay many versions of these adventures. They play a seemingly endless variety of game levels. With unlimited adventures, the holodeck seemingly requires unlimited storage space.

Besides the storage problem, why are the templates, even if stored and retrieved and displayed, never shown too rapidly or slowly? A character might jerk, wobble, or pass accidentally through a wall, dip his feet accidentally through some rocks. Lips might be out of sync with words. Leaves will flutter incorrectly. These types of slipups occur in some of today's best three-dimensional artificially intelligent games.

Yet the holodeck never seems to make mistakes.

The worlds of the holodeck are beyond anything possible today, perhaps even three hundred years from now. Even the greatest computer programs can't function at a speed fast enough to simulate such complex worlds. In virtual reality, there are always program glitches, yet we don't see these frame-skipping glitches and three-dimensional mind-destroying vision-klunking problems in any holodeck simulation. The virtual reality is always seamless. And when holodeck programs do malfunction, they always go off into some artificially intelligent routine that places the real people in danger instead of merely displaying fuzzy pictures or disjointed frames. If virtual reality programming is this sophisticated in three hundred years, then a malfunctioning holodeck adventure would just shut down.

Adding to the holodeck's complexity, replicator technology is routinely used to create inanimate objects to further the illusion of reality. For example, food and drink are served at holodeck bars. There's also water for swimming and snow for throwing snowballs. While many crewmembers enter the holodeck already dressed for their interactive novels, the holodeck can create the proper clothing for participants, as it does in *First Contact*.

The holodeck has treadmill-style force fields so crewmembers can walk and run for long periods. The holographic images keep this illusion of movement believable. The computer program controlling the holodeck operates enough of these specialized force fields that different people can actually feel that they are traveling in opposite directions. The code necessary to maintain such an illusion is obviously quite complex. But it isn't impossible.

Even today we can code repulsion-type forces into virtual objects. Programming statements enable us to ensure that certain objects never collide, that virtual reality characters don't pass through walls. We can make objects attract one another. We can make objects attract and repulse, given changes in position, distance, and size.

Particle systems, another aspect of three-dimensional animation coding, use forces such as gravity and repulsion to simulate blizzards, fireworks, and explosions. For example, we might spray fire from a volcano, then apply a gravitation and repulsion force, making the fire fall at what appears to be a graceful and natural pace.

When we observe the holodeck, we see branches moving, leaves blowing in the wind. Clouds move across the sky. The holodecks are constructed to make everything look natural, with complex systems simulating a natural environment. This requires tons of computing power. But such programs also require an interface for touch, to feel breezes blowing. Do the crewmembers have chips embedded in their fingers so they can feel leaves, weapons, and other objects? Such notions are never mentioned. So how do people feel things and pick up holographic items in the holodeck? What does Captain Picard feel while riding a holographic horse?

In the *Star Trek* universe, important characters who directly interact with crewmembers are made of replicated matter guided by beams of force operating at molecular levels. However, according to the doctor in *Voyager*, the matter is not made of molecules, but rather of molecule-sized magnetic bubbles, which can be manipulated by the computer. These creations are artificially intelligent marionettes whose every motion is controlled by the holodeck's computer system. They're complete with touch, warmth, body sensations, kissing, smiles from the lovers, and violence from the killers. The holodeck magnetic bubble matter that makes up these puppets is described as partially stable stuff that can't exist in material form outside the holodeck.

The holodeck computer is connected with the ship's computer, and thus has access to the vast amounts of information stored in the computer core. The holodeck is capable of creating artificially intelligent imaginary characters (such as Dr. Moriarty in "Elementary, My Dear Data," *TNG*) or artificially intelligent versions of real people programmed with their own personalities, such as Dr. Lea Brahms in the *Next Generation* episode "Booby Trap," or Dr. Zimmerman in *Voyager*. The holodeck can even be used to create artificially intelligent versions of real people with altered personalities.

Transporter and replicator technology are fascinating topics but, as we've noted earlier, appear to be impossible by the laws of physics. Magnetic bubbles the size of molecules fall into physics. None of these topics involve computer technology other than in secondary areas such as memory storage. The artificial intelligence exhibited by the holodeck creations is our main concern.

For the holodeck to create a truly believable environment, two types of interaction are necessary. One requires some sort of interaction between the virtual reality characters; while the other involves interaction between these holodeck beings and real people.

In the first case, that of interaction among the virtual characters, *Star Trek* does a good job of using virtual reality programming as it's perceived today. The typical holodeck characters really don't communicate much with each other beyond preprogrammed gestures and relationships. Perhaps they pass information to each other via their data structures. If one flinches, the flinch probably is an event picked up by the other virtual characters.

We'll return to the possibilities of other, more interesting relationships among virtual holodeck characters. But first let's turn our attention to the interactions between holodeck characters and humans.

Think about Minuet and Riker in the French bar ("11001001," *TNG*). She seems to react realistically to Riker's remarks, moods, and expressions. She acts completely human.

How does this happen?

Most likely, the holodeck computer has sensors that pick up information about the human, in this case, Riker. The holodeck sensors (microscopic and in the walls, as we described in Chapter 2) follow Riker as he moves across the room, detect all of his body movements, and take note of his facial expressions.

If Riker wants to kiss Minuet, the holodeck can detect increased pressure from his lips (as with the treadmill), and then apply force from the virtual Minuet to Riker's lips using a feedback loop of sorts. Though again, it seems that Riker would need microscopic computers embedded in his body, or some other sort of computer mechanism, to receive the feedback sensations and communicate information to his biological components. In other words, the holodeck computer needs a way to communicate Minuet's lip pressure back to Riker's lips. Since it must take considerably more energy to generate molecule-sized magnetic bubbles than a simple visual image, perhaps the computer only creates those parts of Minuet's body that Riker is "touching" at any moment. But it would require extraordinary processing power to create the required textures (both surface and "internal") in real time. And what about smells? Does the computer also create magnetic-bubble perfume?

Minuet may react to Riker simply based on his facial and body expressions. The holodeck computer not only senses but also interprets changes in Riker's expressions. If he smiles and his eyes glow with intense passion, the holodeck computer might interpret his expression as lust. Minuet reacts accordingly. If Riker frowns, glares, bangs his fist on the bar, sinks to the bar top, moans . . . then perhaps the holodeck computer interprets his expressions and actions as depression or anger. If Minuet has just said something that made him sad, then the computer might now have Minuet apologize and cheer him up.

So while Minuet seems almost human, her responses are merely a combination of advanced programming and artificial intelligence. She's not alive, just code.

To be absolutely believable, virtual humans would need to possess many features already built into Data. And this would create new scenarios and adventures, some of which might cause problems.

For example, virtual characters would have to be free to follow their instincts and make their own choices. They'd have to believe that they're real, as opposed to acting as the holodeck computer's puppets. They'd have to learn and grow in their abilities and skills, in their behaviors and personalities. Perhaps they could program new holodeck adventures for themselves, so they could increase their knowledge base. To be artificially intelligent, as defined in Chapter 5, the holodeck characters require a lot of attributes they don't currently have (barring a few exceptions, such as Dr. Moriarty).

If the characters achieve this new level of artificial intelligence, then the holodeck adventures would become much more dangerous. Perhaps this is why they operate exclusively as puppets for the humans.

For example, they might start bickering amongst themselves. They might pursue personal goals. They might form alliances, start wars or become insane.

If Dr. Moriarty can achieve true sentience, why doesn't this happen to lots of holodeck characters?* As with Data, it seems bizarre that only one such creature exists in the entire universe.

In all cases other than Moriarty, we're forced to conclude that characters on the holodeck are not true artificially intelligent virtual reality beings. They lack the required attributes. They're preprogrammed. Only when the ship's computer breaks down in certain episodes do these marionettes ever seem to take on life of their own. Which, we must point out, is pretty unbelievable. Why would preprogrammed actors suddenly be gifted with free will by an energy anomaly?

While the holodeck bars and lounges might be fun, a steady diet of the programs would most likely become boring, predictable, and unreal. Despite Riker's fascination with Minuet, we suspect he'd quickly find her less interesting than Deanna Troi. Captain Janeway's interaction with Leonardo da Vinci is based at least in part on her fascination with his work and life. Interacting with such characters can't offer unpredictability and surprises that only can be provided by real humans (or truly artificially intelligent creatures such as Data).

While the holodeck characters are good for a quick boost, a pulse of sexual arousal, they would be as bland, in the long run, as today's two-dimensional fantasy and pornographic images. Sure, certain people would be hooked on the holodecks for escapism. Those filled with self doubt, for example, might turn to fantasy lives and retreat from reality; might prefer relationships with fake holodeck characters who offer predictable and nonthreatening

---

*Even the recreation of Seska who plagues Tom Paris and Tuvok in "Worst Case Scenario" (*VGR*), is merely a holodeck simulation of the real person, and basically follows a narrow set of commands—torment then kill the two crewmembers.

responses. But most people, especially those who qualify to enter the ranks of Starfleet, would use holodecks for diversion in the same way that most people today use film and magazines. Despite the availability of holosuite fantasy sex, we suspect that the best erotic uses of the holodeck are shared ones.

The ways in which Picard and crew use the holodeck are acceptable, not damaging to their careers, and simply bland amusement. The holodeck novels would be entertaining during their initial run-through, much like the interactive video and computer games available now. Fighting your way through *Beowulf* and slaying monsters definitely could be exciting, even knowing you can't be harmed ("Heroes and Demons," *VGR*). So would be trying to stop a mutiny with the lives of your friends at stake ("Worst Case Scenario," *VGR*).

But, as with games today, we suspect that once the game was complete, the *Trek* user wouldn't bother playing again. For all their exotic backgrounds, holodeck novels are still only stories, not real life.

Dr. Moriarty complains about this very fact—that his life in storage is deadly sterile and boring. He wants freedom.

Missing Bits

As we've noted, *Star Trek* in all its incarnations is much less an extrapolation of advanced science than a projection of today's culture three hundred years into the future. Thus the computers on the ship are merely faster versions of what we have today. Weapons like photon torpedoes are more destructive renditions of today's technology. Each *Star Trek* series is a product of its times.

So far, we've concentrated on the areas where *Star Trek* and reality intersect. But not all of our future is in *Star Trek*. Much is neglected or ignored. It's time to take a look at where our world and the universe of television diverge. The stuff that's missing or just plain wrong.

The Borg

If Vaal and Landru, the giant supercomputers of the original series, symbolize the 1960s' fear of automation, then the Borg are the ultimate late twentieth-century bogeymen. They're an updated Frankenstein's monster, computer technology gone berserk, the sentient machine overwhelming its outdated master. Like Vaal, the Borg give voice to our concern about our growing dependence on computers in our daily lives. Instead of humanity becoming a slave to the machine as in the original series, we're faced with the horrifying possibility of mankind *becoming* the machine.

The Collective isn't user friendly. The Borg consider humans "irrelevant." We're face to face with the relentless, cold logic of the computer. The Borg are so frightening not for what they are but for what they predict about us and where society is going.

One of the best examples of Borg as Frankenstein monsters is in the movie *First Contact*. The Borg are banging on the sick bay door, trying to hammer it down. Dr. Crusher activates the Emergency Medical Holograph program. When the holographic doctor appears, Crusher tells him to create a diversion. In true *Trek* doctor form, he protests, "I'm a doctor, not a doorstop." But then, noting that implants can cause skin irritations, he asks the twenty Borg who bang into sick bay: "Perhaps you'd like an analgesic cream?" The monsters stagger around like Halloween ghouls while the humans race for their lives. It's a marvelous scene.

The Borg are the perfect villains for our computer age. Unlike the Dominion in *Deep Space Nine*, they don't seek to rule other worlds, forge alliances for conquest, or negotiate treaties. Instead, they have only one goal: to assimilate other species into the Collective, to transform all they meet into Borg. There's no compromise with the Borg. They're quite clear when they state, "We are the Borg. You will be assimilated. *Resistance is futile.*" Again, the underlying fear is that people must deal with a computerized society whether they like it or not.

That the Borg are quite successful is evident by what little has been revealed about them. Located primarily in the Delta Quadrant of the galaxy, they control thousands of solar systems that stretch for several thousand light years. Twice they've attacked Federation space, using just one ship, and both times were barely defeated. An attack fleet of hundreds of Borg cubes could undoubtedly wipe out human civilization.

According to Q, the Borg are neither male nor female but enhanced humanoids sharing a collective mind with no single leader. They are the ultimate biological/machine interface ("Q Who?" *TNG*). Using subspace neural-link transceivers, they instantly transmit information among all minds in the Collective. Thus, all Borg form one communal mind—a mind that controls great forces and is capable of tremendous healing power ("Unity," *VGR*).

One glaring inconsistency in this description is the Borg Queen (*Star Trek: First Contact*). A supreme Borg ruler (or even a group of such rulers) makes no sense. The collective hive intelligence blends the thoughts and knowledge of all minds of the individual members. No one person directs the action of all. The decisions are made by all, for all. That is one of the reasons severe casualties cannot stop the Borg. Their strength resides in the group.

Locutus served as a mouthpiece for the Borg to communicate with humans. So did Seven of Nine. Neither drone controlled the Collective. They were merely extensions of it.

The Borg Queen made good theater. It was a lot easier for viewers to focus on a villain rather than a hive-mind that made decisions based on the input of all its members. But when she claims in *First Contact* to "bring order to chaos," she becomes nothing more than an illogical plot device. The *Star Trek* writers seem to have fallen into the trap of thinking that if the Collective is conscious, that consciousness must be *located* somewhere within it. But this makes no sense. Consider your brain, which (we hope) is undoubtedly conscious. Is your consciousness located in just one part of your brain? Suppose you start removing cells from that part. The individual cells are not conscious; at some point you arrive at a structure where consciousness is a property of the whole but not of any of its parts. How big is the whole? Perhaps it's not your brain but your *whole body* that's conscious. In the same way, the consciousness of the Collective is much more likely to reside in the whole than in any of its "cells."

For the Borg, to think is virtually to act. When their ship is damaged by the *Enterprise-D* photon torpedoes, the Borg regenerate the damage by merely thinking about it ("Q Who?" *TNG*). As one huge mind, the Collective often ignores small details or events while focusing on performing specific, more important tasks. In many ways, the Borg resemble a network of parallel linked computers.

The Borg begin as biological life forms (as shown in the ship's nursery in "Q Who?"), but soon after birth, are connected to the Collective through artificially intelligent implants. Humans and other intelligent life forms are assimilated through injections of Borg nanoprobes that convert them into members of the group mind. This process occurs very quickly, as shown by Captain Picard's conversion into Locutus in *The Next Generation* episode "The Best of Both Worlds" and the assimilation of various members of the *Enterprise-E* crew in *First Contact*. Again, the parallels between our growing dependence on computers, from early childhood onward, is obvious.

In his study of the Borg nanoprobes, the holographic doctor on *Voyager* comments on the amazing speed at which the nanotech devices attack human blood cells. And he marvels at how the mechanisms used to inject those nanoprobes can pierce any armor ("Scorpion," *VGR*). The Borg, like modern technological advances, are seemingly unstoppable.

It's pretty unbelievable that nanotechnology's been developed by the Borg and not by the Federation. Nanoprobes are sophisticated scientific devices, not something that a holographic computer program can cook up in a few weeks. There needs to be a huge library of information and background available for Dr. Crusher to propose using nanotechnology against the Borg—or even to estimate that it would take three weeks to develop nanites to fight the invaders. Twenty-one days isn't enough time to develop an entirely new branch of science.

Still, nanotechnology seems to lurk in the shadows of Federation research. Wesley accidentally creates a nanotech civilization in "Evolution" (*TNG*). In "Ethics" (*TNG*), Worf receives neurotransducers, nano-implants that pick up his brain's electrical signals and stimulate the appropriate muscles. He also receives an entirely new spinal column, cooked up for him in a vat within a day. If Federation doctors can remove a spinal column and boil up a new one in a kettle, and toss in a few hundred or thousand nano-implants to make it work, then Federation science already knows a heck of a lot about nanotechnology.

Yet it's never used in any intelligent way.

In *The Next Generation*'s "I, Borg," an analysis of Three of Five's biochip implants provides a great deal of information about the Borg command structure. An invasive code is developed on the *Enterprise* that is deemed capable of destroying the entire Borg Collective, but it's never implemented. Why this code isn't used when the Borg attack Earth in *First Contact* isn't clear.

In *First Contact*, Picard kills two Borg using a holodeck machine gun from the 1930s. We wonder of course how a holographic gun can kill anyone.* But this objection aside, it's unlikely that a bullet could kill a Borg. Surely their nanotech devices repair the creatures and regenerate lost tissues. A bullet wound shouldn't be a big deal to nanotechnology this sophisticated. But most implausible is Picard's statement that each Borg has a neu-

---

*It's possible to beam real guns and weapons into the holodeck, but that doesn't seem to happen in this episode. (In any case, it's unlikely that the *Enterprise* weapons locker would have a few 1930s Tommy guns and perhaps a musket or two stashed behind the phaser rifles.)

roprocessor: "It's like a memory chip. It'll contain the record of all the instructions this Borg has been receiving from the Collective." If it's so easy to decode the neuroprocessor device, why hasn't the Federation disabled all Borg neuroprocessors using destruction commands sent over wireless transmissions?

It's because the Borg are just too much fun to remove them from the show. And so, as fans, we ignore their illogical aspects. Just as we ignore the medical improbabilities that abound in all the *Trek* adventures.

◀ Medicine ▮▮▮▮▮▮▮▮▮▮▮▮▮▮▮▮▮▮▮▮▮▮▮▮ ▷

Doctors play an important part in the *Star Trek* universe. Dr. McCoy in the original series, Drs. Crusher and Pulaski in *The Next Generation*, Dr. Bashir in *Deep Space Nine*, and the holographic doctor in *Voyager* are all dedicated, hard-working individuals (if sometimes lacking in bedside manner) and superb physicians who perform medical miracles undreamed of in our time.

Or do they? Is the medical technology of *Star Trek* that advanced? Most pertinent for this book, are computers as integrated into the healing arts as fully as they should be in the world of the future?

Again, we find recycled, outdated concepts pushed ahead three hundred years. Like Landru and its smoking vacuum tubes, what's true in medicine today won't necessarily be true centuries from now, just as much of the basic healing lore of three centuries ago is seen as superstitious nonsense today. Too much of *Star Trek's* medical technology is merely unimaginative projections of today's doctoring tossed bodily into the future.

Consider tricorders. They've been featured in *Star Trek* from the very first series. As demonstrated throughout hundreds of episodes, a tricorder is used as a computer, a sensor, and a portable communicator for immediate contact with the starship or other crewmembers. It's operated by touch but also responds to voice commands. In many ways, they're like the PADDs discussed in Chapter 2. At the time of the first series, tricorders were quite futuristic, a remarkably accurate guess of what was to come.

The medical tricorder, used by Dr. McCoy and all who followed him, is just a standard tricorder with a number of additional functions. Medical tricorders are primarily used to scan crewmembers for organ system functions, diseases, and other health problems. Tricorders have huge memories (isolinear chips, of course) and so hold huge amounts of information in their medical databases.

Impossible today? At this moment, yes, but medical tricorders aren't very far in the future. Hospitals are relying more and more on handheld computer devices to measure everything from body temperature (a sensor placed in the patient's ear for an instant) to blood pressure (done on one finger). Twenty or thirty years from now, we can expect hospital personnel to be carrying medical tricorders, capable of performing numerous medical tasks, as part of their standard equipment.

Biobeds are used routinely in all the *Star Trek* series. Victims of accidents, disease, and attacks are placed there for recovery. The beds monitor all major life systems and include a variety of surgical support frames. Science fiction? Only in the slightest sense of the word. Check out the Intensive Care Unit of any major hospital. Computers are used to monitor patients' vital signs. Emergency equipment for dealing with everything from choking to heart attacks is on hand. The only difference between the beds on *Star Trek* and those today is the absence of the wires used for sensors. While perhaps not as tightly linked with computers, critical-care units are quickly approaching that standard.

More to the point, the biobeds on *Trek* are merely extensions of medical technology that's been around for years. They're nothing new or different. *Star Trek*'s view of the future of medicine is bland and remarkably short-sighted.

When Worf's badly injured in an accident, shattering seven of his vertebrae and crushing his spinal cord, he's told he'll probably be permanently paralyzed ("Ethics," *TNG*). Dr. Toby Russell, a neurogeneticist consulted by Dr. Crusher, wants to use an experimental nanotech medical technique to repair the damage. She does so, though Dr. Crusher feels that Russell is taking unnecessary risks with patient's lives.

More than three centuries from now, and nanotechnology is still experimental? How then does the Doctor on *Voyager* solve the Borg's problem with Species 8472 in just a few weeks? His solution requires a detailed knowledge of nanoprobes and how to modify them. Yet a crushed spinal cord can't be repaired by Federation science using this same technology. Remember, this is the same world in which science has cured heart disease, liver damage, and emphysema ("The Neutral Zone," *TNG*) and can bring back to life people who died from those problems. Not logical, as Mr. Spock might suggest.

Speaking of Spock, when Dr. McCoy needs to operate on his father, Sarek, the doctor complains he's never done surgery on a Vulcan before ("Journey to Babel," *TOS*). Since the *Enterprise* computer core holds nearly all the information in the Federation, shouldn't it contain detailed information about how to conduct such an operation? Or why not check a computer operation simulator, as developed by the Swiss Federal Institute of Technology, capable of reproducing operations in virtual reality environments, so the doctor could run through the operation before attempting it?[1]

Or, if Dr. McCoy needs some expert advice, why not use subspace communication to discuss his problems with doctors on Vulcan? Similar consultations took place in 1993, in Mogadishu, Somalia, when specialists broadcast pictures of medical problems they couldn't solve from a tent hospital and received answers from all over the world by phone and fax.[2]

Again, the future of medicine looks a lot different from what's shown on *Trek*. Where, for instance, are the "smart-shirts"? "Smart-Shirts" are garments developed with funding from the Department of Defense Advanced Research Projects Agency. They look like ordinary t-shirts (or *Star Trek* uniforms) but have plastic optic fibers and other special fibers sewn into the material and computer processors built into the clothing. The shirts are already being called "one of the genuine breakthroughs for the next century" by one of its inventors, Sundaresan Jayaraman of the Georgia Institute of Technology.[3]

The fibers in the shirt work together to create a network of data about the wearer's health. Sensors send information on heartbeat, breathing, and other vital signs to a miniature processor worn on the user's belt. This information can be sent by satellite anywhere on Earth.

The shirts can immediately detect heart attacks. Or sense heat buildup on the skin, alerting firefighters to possible flashpoints in buildings.

More astonishing, these "smart-shirts" can even monitor bullet wounds. When a bullet tears through the fiber, the location is immediately noted by the network of optic mesh throughout the shirt. Incredibly thin microphones in the material record sound waves as the bullet passes through the victim's body, creating a digital picture of how deep and where the slug went. Such information is then immediately sent by satellite to doctors, and medics can be immediately dispatched to the scene of the shooting. In the meantime, sensors also detect whether blood is coming from a vein or artery.

Perhaps the most amazing fact about these "smart-shirts" is that they cost approximately $30. While not yet licensed for public use (they're still in the final development stage for the Army), there's little doubt that they will become available to the general public within the next few years. At first, they will probably be used mainly for elderly people in poor health or in nursing homes. But as their sensors become more refined, they will undoubtedly become popular garments for anyone suffering any type of health risk as well as for athletes and others who want to monitor their own cardiovascular functions.

Real-life computer medical technology is quickly outpacing *Star Trek*. Pushing the concept of "smart-shirts" three centuries into the future would give us uniforms that would not only protect the crew but heal them when injured. But *Trek* medicine is both too conservative and too melodramatic. Such as when it comes to plagues.

With the advances in medicine over the past hundred years, epidemics are infrequent and quickly isolated and controlled. Despite a plethora of non-fiction books and novels about "hot zones," killer plagues are not breaking out all over the globe. True, the possibility of chemical and biological warfare is a grim reminder of human stupidity. Yet, except for AIDS, the scares that draw headlines in the West—such as mad cow disease or flesh-eating bacteria—result from small numbers of actual cases. But, that seems not to apply to our *Star Trek* future.

The crew of the original series encounter more than their share of plagues and killer viruses. In "The Naked Time," a landing party sent to the planet Psi 2000 discovers that the science team stationed there are all dead. Though the investigators from the *Enterprise* are wearing protective gear, one crewmember has a bad itch on his chin and removes his gloves to scratch, thus becoming infected with the deadly virus. (This scratching moment has to be one of the most embarrassingly stupid scenes ever in a *Star Trek* episode.)

In the original series episode "Miri," an away team discovers a destroyed civilization on a planet much like Earth. Here, an experiment to prolong life has resulted in a plague that killed off the adult population, while slowing the aging of the children to one month per century.

And on a mission to the Gamma Hydra IV research colony, the crew discovers all the colonists dead or dying of an aging disease. Needless to say, the disease soon strikes the crew. McCoy, as usual, develops an antidote in the nick of time ("The Deadly Years").

In three years of the original series, there are eight encounters with killer diseases. While we realize that some colonies are not fully established, it seems hard to believe that they don't have medical facilities capable of handling these emergencies. In any case, do the vaccines have to be delivered by hand? Can't formulas be sent via subspace? And what about a comprehensive medical library containing the chemical formulas necessary for synthesizing of the vaccines?

While deadly infections are less common in *The Next Generation*, they still occur with alarming frequency. Early in their explorations, Picard et al. rendezvous with the science vessel *Tsiolkovsky* only to find all eighty of its crew dead. They've been killed by a virus similar to the notorious Psi 2000 disease. Once again, the away team brings the infection back to the crew of the *Enterprise* ("The Naked Now").

Several months later, the *Enterprise* is sent to transport specimens of a plasma plague to a science station in hopes of finding a cure for an epidemic on the planet Rachelis ("The Child"). Soon after, the *Enterprise* receives a distress call from the starship Lantree. The crew of the ship is found dead, from what looks like old age. It's another deadly virus, this time an artificial one, caused by genetically engineered children with powerful immune systems ("Unnatural Selection").

We could go on.

Actually, these incidents aren't surprising when we consider away-team policies on *Star Trek*. In all of the various *Trek* series, we're treated to scene after scene of people beaming down to a planet without any protective gear. When they return, rarely are they put in quarantine before being allowed to roam the ship. Presumably this is because the transporter contains a "biofilter" that screens out alien microbes—but it is clearly not 100 percent reliable. In *Trek*, it's easier to visit a totally unknown planet than it is for a traveler today to go to Africa or Asia.

Medicine today is incredibly advanced from what it was only fifty years ago, much less centuries past. New discoveries are being made constantly, and there is no reason to believe that the next few decades will not be filled with even more startling advances. Given the state of medical technology three centuries from now, combined with the tremendous speed and memory of computers, it's hard to believe that so many infections will present greater problems than the cuts and scrapes Dr. Crusher heals with her "dermal regenerator." Infectious microbes survive by making copies of themselves—which means that the members of a strain of microbes will be pretty much identical. They'll all have the same surface chemistry. The body's natural immune system works by identifying particular chemicals (called "antigens") on the surfaces of microbes, and synthesizing complementary proteins, called antibodies, to attack them. Any infectious agent—fungus, bacteria, virus, prion, or even something totally alien—is bound to have *some* consistent chemical signature by which it can be distinguished from the body's own tissues. Three hundred years from now, there will certainly be a common computer algorithm that will analyze this signature, design a molecule that can serve as an artificial antibody and provide instructions for its rapid synthesis. Then these molecules can be attached to nanites and injected into the bloodstream.

Many diseases, such as the AIDS virus or the malaria parasite, remain deadly by periodically changing their surface antigens. They may change, but nanites can change faster.

◀ Universal Translators ███████████████ ▶

I t's well documented that Gene Roddenberry came up with the idea of transporters for the original series, because landing a huge starship like the *Enterprise* on a planet's surface every week would break the show's limited budget. Entering and leaving shuttlecraft would waste valuable running time. Thus one of the most fascinating (though absolutely impossible[4]) concepts in science-fiction television was born.

That's often the case with television and the movies. Budget and time constraints force compromises in plot and logic. There are only so many minutes to tell a story. It's why in the original *Mission Impossible*, characters were seen opening doors to corridors but never walking through them. Save those seconds for more important scenes. On *Star Trek*, considering that week after week the crew is encountering new races, dealing with interstellar crises, and defending themselves against unimaginable menaces, it's not surprising that there are shortcuts. Transporters, the holographic doctor, and replicators are shortcuts. So are computer communicators and Universal Translators.

Why is it so easy for starships from different interstellar empires to establish communications? Why are the messages from the Klingons, Cardassians and the Romulans so similar? They frequently even sign off in the same manner. There seems to be an implicit assumption that Starfleet officers can not only use but hack any computer they find, and breaking codes is child's play for Data. Encrypted messages are routinely intercepted and deciphered during the war with the Dominion.

Examples of computer compatibility abound in all series. The Gorm send a false message to the *Enterprise*, luring crewmembers into a trap on the planet Cestus ("Arena," *TOS*). Khan Noonien Singh has no problems using the *Enterprise's* computers, even after three centuries of improvement ("Space Seed," *TOS*). Spock's brain is stolen from his body and used as a CPU in the computer system of Sigma Draconis VI ("Spock's Brain," *TOS*).

In *The Next Generation*, the Bynars steal the *Enterprise* to use its main computer to restart their computerized civilization ("11001001"). An automated computerized weapon system almost destroys the *Enterprise* while advertising its superior weaponry ("The Arsenal of Freedom").

It's the same in all the shows. Garak manages to rework Dominion technology to save himself and friends from captivity on a prison asteroid ("In Purgatory's Shadow," *DS9*). Sisko pilots a captured Jem'Hadar starship in a sneak attack on one of their bases ("Rocks and Shoals," *DS9*). And a being in the form of a spatial-distortion ring downloads 20 million gigaquads of information into *Voyager's* computer memory banks ("Twisted," *VGR*).

These are interstellar confederations that have existed for centuries, even millennia. Many races, such as the Vulcans, were traveling through interstellar space long before warp drive was developed on Earth (*First Contact*). The Borg have been evolving for more than a thousand centuries. Yet obtaining information files and software is commonplace between Federation members. And their enemies! There's no problem involving executable systems. Even in the Delta Quadrant, far from the Federation, the crew of *Voyager* seems to have no difficulty communicating and trading with the dozens of new races they encounter.

Which forces us to ask the obvious question. Is some galactic Microsoft selling Windows 2400 to every computer user in the universe? Are we looking at another television shortcut like the transporters? Or is it actually possible that the computer systems of the many races of the *Star Trek* universe might somehow be compatible? In *The Next Generation* episode, "The Chase," we're informed that many of the humanoid species in the galaxy are the result of genetic seeding done by an ancient humanoid race millions of years ago. Could this interrelationship between Earthlings, Klingons, Romulans, and others be in some way responsible for the similarity of their computer technology? It's a fascinating theory, almost mystical, that shared genetic codes can lead to parallel developments in science. But there's another possible—though improbable—explanation.

As we explained early in this book, computers in their most basic form are merely collections of on-off switches. The on-off position is determined by the flow of electricity through a transistor. Each transistor represents one bit of data. Group a number of bits together and you form a byte, a basic unit of information for a computer. Link millions, or billions of bytes together, add an operating system, and you have a computer.

What's important is that all digital computers depend on bits—on whether a switch is on or off, as determined by the flow of electricity. Computers are not dependent on human or alien languages, the appearance of their operators or the location of their home world. They're based on one of the basic truisms of physics, the flow of electrons.

Thus, the Bynars, ("11001001," *TNG*) even though they are an alien race who evolved independently of Terran civilization, use digital computers, based on the same basic concept of digital computers—binary language. And they're described as the finest computer engineers in the Alpha Quadrant. Once we accept the idea that binary codes and bits are a likely path for development of computers, it stops being totally unbelievable that the various cybernetic systems used by the different races in the galaxy might have a basic common denominator.

Which raises the question: Are there possible computer systems not dependent on binary machine language? At least one *Star Trek* race uses computers that are totally different from anything used in our galaxy. That's because the aliens who employ them aren't from our universe. They come from fluidic space and are supposedly the ultimate biological creations. The Borg call them Species 8472 and their starships and computers are composed entirely from organic matter ("Scorpion, Parts 1 and 2," *VGR*). Where the Federation's computers use optical switches as the heart of their processors, Species 8472's computers use DNA, the genetic material of living cells.

Is such a thing possible? In fact, DNA computers have been in the works for years. In 1997, two researchers at the University of Rochester, Animesh Ray and Mitsu Ogihara, constructed logic gates using DNA molecules, a major step towards DNA computers capable of solving problems normally handled by digital computers. DNA computers seem a very real part of our future.

Instead of using silicon chips and electrical currents, DNA computers rely on deoxyribonucleic acids—A (adenine), C (cytosine), G (guanine) and T (thymine)—as memory units and carry out fundamental operations by recombinant techniques. The main difference between DNA computers and electronic computers is that regular computer bits have two positions (On/Off) while DNA bits have four (C, G, A, and T). Therefore, DNA molecules can in theory handle any problem done on a conventional computer, but can also manage more complex operations as well by using their extra two positions.

As we've discussed earlier in this book, most electronic computers handle operations linearly—one operation at a time, though at incredible speeds. DNA computers rely on biochemical reactions that work in parallel. A single operation in a DNA computer can affect trillions of other DNA strands. DNA computers are thus much faster than any electronic computer.

Synthesized DNA strands are used in DNA computers. The amount of information that can be stored in these biological strands is staggering. One cubic centimeter of DNA material can hold as much as 1021 bits of information. More to the point, it's estimated that one pound of synthetic DNA has the capacity to store more information than all the electronic computers in use in the world today.

Needless to say, future advances in DNA computers hold great promise. At present, they're only capable of solving very specific types of logic problems, but it seems quite likely that in three centuries, fully functional DNA computers will be a reality. Their existence on the biological ships of Species 8472 is much closer than three centuries in the future.

With their totally incompatible computer systems, communication between *Voyager* and Species 8472 is impossible. (Fortunately, Kes' telepathic powers come to the rescue. Never underestimate psychic power when you need a deus ex machina.) Usually, when *Voyager* or any other Federation starship makes contact with a new alien species, the Universal Translator comes into play. It's another wonderful time-saving device that eliminates a lot of dead air (although the hilarious scene in *The Undiscovered Country* in which the *Enterprise's* bridge crew all crowd around Uhura, leafing frantically through dusty old English-Klingon dictionaries because they think the Klingon outpost they're trying to slip past would be made suspicious by the Universal Translator, is an anachronism not to be missed). Still, while a Universal Translator sounds like a necessary tool for any space exploration team, is it really possible?

Maybe, but not as presented on *Trek*. Present day computers are capable of roughly translating documents from one language to another in seconds. Hand-held computers have been developed to translate words spoken in one language to another. It won't be long before telephone calls made between different countries will feature automatic translation. In all these cases, however, we're working with two known languages and two known sets of grammatical rules. That won't be the case if and when we encounter alien species in outer space.

According to *The Star Trek: The Next Generation—Technical Manual,* the Universal Translator is a very sophisticated computer program that analyzes patterns of unknown languages and then comes up with a system to translate our speech into that language. This is done by obtaining large samples of aliens speaking with each other, so the program can study usage patterns, vocabulary, syntax and so on. It all sounds very logical. Too bad it makes no sense.

Computers are wonderful code-breakers, the finest such devices in the universe. But languages are not codes. Conversations without reference points do not necessarily illuminate what they are about. For example, try watching a Japanese film without subtitles. When two Samurai meet in a noodle shop, are they discussing the weather, the best way to kill a man, the politics of the town, whether the girl serving them noodles is attractive, or the meaning of the universe? Any of these conversations is equally possible, and they all sound quite similar. Japanese can't be learned by assembling a huge library of conversations and then analyzing them by a computer. It's like the 1950s science-fiction movies where the aliens claim to have learned to speak English by watching our television shows. Unfortunately *I Love Lucy* doesn't work as a language primer. Something more is necessary. A key. A Rosetta stone.

When humans encounter an alien race, there is not automatically a third species that knows both languages and can serve as a bridge between them. Nor is every race in *Star Trek* telepathic (though for simplicity's sake, it seems that an awful lot of them are!). Are we forced to conclude that the Universal Translator is no more than a neat gimmick? Not entirely but almost.

In the classic science-fiction story "Omnilingual," by H. Beam Piper,[5] the author addresses the problem of translating an alien language into English. Making it even more difficult on the archaeologists, the language in question is Martian and the inhabitants of the red planet have been dead for forty thousand years, leaving behind a ruined civilization. The question raised in the story is pretty much the same we are faced with in the Universal Translator. How do you decipher an alien language without a tongue common to both civilizations? Piper came up with the answer and it's as true now as it was forty years ago and will be true three centuries in the future. Science and mathematics.

Despite differences in culture, society, philosophy, and patterns of speech among civilizations, our atomic table of elements is always the same. The atomic structure of water, H_2O, is identical everywhere in the universe. The sum of $2 + 2 = 4$ cannot change. The basic laws of physics and mathematics are the same throughout the universe. They form a universal language.

Using basic building blocks of scientific and mathematical terminology, a fairly detailed dictionary of words can be constructed. With AI computers, working at incredible speeds, extrapolating terms dealing with the manipulation of such words would follow quickly. In days, perhaps hours, a simple but useful glossary could be constructed, and from there, with continued dialogue between species, a true Universal Translator could be devised.

That's not the way it's done on *Star Trek*. At least, we never see it handled in such a manner. The *Technical Manual* offers us a magic wand but nothing practical. Still, the method we describe is one possible way it might work in the future.

Like many of the devices displayed on *Star Trek*, the Universal Translator is possible. The key is that it must rely on real computer technology and logic. But, like many of the inventions shown on the series, it is coming. The *Star Trek* future is on the way. Most likely, sooner than we think.

Chapter One

1. "More Storage, Please," by Mark Halper, http://www.forbes.com, July 7, 1997.

Chapter Two

1. Rick Sternach and Michael Okuda, *Star Trek: The Next Generation—Technical Manual* (New York: Pocket Books, 1991).

2. David A. Patterson and John L. Hennessy, *Computer Architecture: A Quantitative Approach* (San Mateo, CA: Morgan Kaufmann Publishers, Inc., 1990). See pages 199–201 for a quick introduction to processors.

3. *Star Trek: The Next Generation—Technical Manual*, page 49.

4. Ibid.

5. Ibid.

6. Rick Sternach and Michael Okuda, *Star Trek Encyclopedia: A Reference Guide to the Future* (New York: Pocket Books, 1997).

7. "More Storage, Please," *Forbes*, July 7, 1997.

8. Ibid.

Chapter Three

1. "Onward Cyber Soldiers," by Douglas Waller and Mark Thomas, *Time,* August 21, 1995, pp. 38–46.

2. http://www.gilc.org/privacy.

3. Bruce Schneier, *Applied Cryptography,* Second Edition (New York: John Wiley & Sons, 1996).

4. Bruce Schneier and David Banisar, *The Electronic Privacy Papers* (New York: John Wiley & Sons, 1997).

5. *Dr. Dobb's Journal,* December 1998.

6. http://www.ddj.com, *Dr. Dobb's Journal,* December 1998, article written by Bruce Schneier.

Chapter Four

1. http://www.stricom.army.mil/.

Chapter Five

1. Rodney Brooks, "Elephants Don't Play Chess," *Robotics and Autonomous Systems,* (North Holland: Elsevier Science Publishers, 1990). Also: Rodney Brooks, "New Approaches to Robotics," *Science,* (September 3, 1991).

Chapter Six

1. http://www.robotstore.com/mwmars.htm.

Chapter Seven

1. Rick Sternach and Michael Okuda, *Star Trek: The Next Generation—Technical Manual* (New York: Pocket Books, 1991).

Chapter Eight

1. Maryann Karinch, *Telemedicine*, (Horizon Press, 1995), Introduction.

2. Ibid.

3. "Smart T-Shirts Know When Something Is Wrong," *USA Today*, 17 November 1998, p. 10D.

4. Lawrence M. Krauss, *The Physics of Star Trek* (New York: Basic Books, 1995).

5. H. Beam Piper, "Omnilingual," *Astounding Science Fiction* (January 1957).

Index